MARITIME
HARWICH
as a ferry port

A miscellany since 986 (or thereabouts)

A
Pictorial
History

by
Harry G. Hitchman
&
Philip Driver

INTRODUCTION

My colleague and I have introduced this book to bridge a few of the gaps that appear in our previous publications, but at the same time we have also aimed to present, between these covers, a book in its own right.

In presenting this illustrated book we have attempted to satisfy the reader's interest in the historical and in the nostalgic. For the purely historical we have indulged in a little English humour with a Viking skit to prove that English history did start before 1066, and all that. From then onwards pure history appears in the true word. For the nostalgic - we trust the photographs of many of the ships which have sailed from the ferry port of Harwich over the past few generations will prove gratifying as they recall more than just the odd memory. For today's traveller the book is presented in a manner so that it may be retained as a life-long souvenir of a journey taken in the comfort and style associated with the present generation of ferry boat - or more appropriately a ferry cruiser/liner. For the reader interested in nautical automation the photographs regarding the transition from paddle ship to oil via the steam ship are the best we can obtain - using the techniques of modern printing. This ensures the greatest clarity available to date.

My colleague, Philip Driver and I, extend grateful thanks to those who have assisted with the make up of this book and to those who have provided the illustrations.

HARRY G. HITCHMAN

Research Assistance: L. Weaver B.A. Curator Harwich Town Archives
                        P. Gates Esq. Curator Harwich Maritime Museum

Photos and Art Material: Nick Aldridge, Henry Allen, DFDS Seaways, Peter Gates,
                           Terry McBurney, Sealink (UK) Ltd., Harwich/Hook Ferry Line,
                           Parkeston Quay, Alfred Smith, Marine photographer, World
                           Ship Society, Manchester.

Edited by: M. Davies B.A.

Published by: Harry G. Hitchman - 19 Wick Lane, Dovercourt, Harwich
                 CO12 3TA

Printed by: Autoprint, Harwich - 504944

Other Books by the Author, include:

'PARKESTON: A century of service' -   First published   March 1983

'HARWICH: - A nautical history' -   First published   June 1984
                                     Re-issued   June 1985

'HMS BADGER: Harwich in the front line' -First published   August 1985

Longships: probably the first ferries to cross the North Sea - 986 (or thereabouts)

A Viking fleet would sail into a river estuary like the Stour which gave Viking raiders, merchants and settlers easy across to the lands and wealth of the Anglo Saxons. When the current grew too strong, or the ships lost the wind, they would fold their sails, lower the mast, and unship the oars, a task that, for a trained crew, should not have taken more than a few minutes. With a combination of sails for the North Sea and oars for the shallow draught of the estuary. Viking ships could adapt themselves to all waters.

986 OR THEREABOUTS ......

Once upon a time, way back in the days of the year 986, new Danish raiders appeared on coasts to the North of East Anglia, then part of the Saxon kingdom ruled by Ethelred, nicknamed "Ethelred the Unready". He like most of his countrymen in those days, was unready to meet this new Danish assault against his country. Instead of the skill shown by Alfred, 100 years earlier, treachery and stupidity now met the invaders. Although in some places here and there resistance was a little firmer against the organized bodies of professional armies commanded by the Kings of Denmark, the Viking raiders still savaged and plundered their way along the coast. Sacking and burning the villages in Northumbria, they struck deep into the countryside. They seized and held vast tracts of land, following up with further invasions to the South.

During one such excursion the Danish fleet rested in a natural harbour, preparing to force their way up rivers in order to cut off the Anglo Saxon forces in Norwich. On this occasion the local inhabitants crept down and burnt the Danish ships. This incurred the wrath of the Danish King and his army, for their mobility depended upon such ships. They promptly forced the local population to rebuild the ships. The Danes established an encampment on the ridge overlooking the harbour, which they named DOVENKORT, (from the Danish - Doven meaning "idle" and Kort "of short duration").

Whilst the locals and the army were engaged in the task of shipbuilding, the King's advisors, having little to do, studied the seas and the weather. They wished to please their monarch saying he would be a great King - one to rule over all the lands and seas. In order to prove this greatness, they had the king seated upon the throne by the sea shore, and asked him to command the seas to go back. The waters did roll back - proving the clever Danes had invented a tide table.

Illustration of Canute the Great: King of England and Denmark, from a print in the Centrum Biblioteket, Aarhus.

3

Canute, astounded by his powers, looked into the Heavens and shouted - "AErling, Odin jeg er stor". (Honest, Odin I am Great). The local Serfs, who had been forced to witness the greatness of the Overlord, remembered his words but could only pronounce the first word as "EArlam". However, this stretch of beach was held in such reverence by the Danes and Saxons, that to this day, there has been erected neither jetty nor quay thereon.

Canute marshalled his armies and rebuilt the fleet in a preparation for a descent on London. The eventual result of these new and relentless attacks swept aside the uncertain resistance of the Anglo Saxons. Ethelred died in London in 1016 whilst Canute's fleet was sailing up the Thames. The country was divided as Ethelred's son, Edmund Ironside, gallantly continued to fight for the Saxon cause. At Ashington in Essex his army clashed in battle with Canute's forces which were marching on London. Edmund Ironside was routed. He became a fugitive and died in London in November 1016- By early next year, the divided country accepted Canute as their ruler. The eventual result was the establishment of a Dane on the Saxon throne.

Canute, anointed with Holy Oil by the Bishops, was so emotionally moved by the Christian attitude of his new subjects, he named the kingdom "Engel land". (Angel Land).

From that day since, despite the changing facits of History, Canute's name for his conquered country was to remain - ENGLAND.

It was in 1086, twenty years after the Battle of Hastings that William, King of Normandy decided to take stock of his captured country - England. His "researchers", in those times known probably as commissioners travelled the length and breath of the land, meeting the headman from each town, village and hamlet who was sworn to tell the truth and nothing but the truth. At that time the country was divided into "hundreds" for domestic purposes. In the hundreds of Tendring in Essex there is an entry for Dovercourt but no mention of Harwich. This can only mean that in 1086 there was nothing worth mentioning where Harwich now stands. A name similar to Harwich i.e., Herwyz first appeared in the thirteenth century. The origin is obscure but it is possible the Danes camped there. The surprising fact was however, that there was no settlement in 1087 - Why not?

However, back to the Doomsday Book where there is an abbreviated entry which can be translated as follows:- "DRUVRECURT". This was an estate owned by Ulwin which was passed on to him by Aubrey in the life of King Edward. There were eight Villeins, there are now in 1086 only six. There were then six borders; there are now twelve. Then there were six Serfs and three ploughs on the estate and six ploughs belonging to the Serfmen. There are three acres of meadow with pastures for twenty sheep. There were then, twelve beasts, 200 sheep and forty swine. These are all now the same. It was then worth six pounds but is now valued at twelve.

Thus it can be seen in those times how the cost of living went up at the end of each war.

It is interesting to note that the estate before 1066 was held by the brother of King Harold who now lost his land to Aubrey, who was to become Earl of Oxford. In those days a Hide was about 120 acres. The estate of Dovercourt covered about 720 acres.

In those days a Villein rented about thirty acres of land and in return worked on it and made 'gifts' of eggs, poultry, honey, cheese etc., as set down in the Court rolls. Besides the regular two or three days of "Week Work" a Villein was liable for extra boon work such as unpaid overtime during harvest and during the haymaking period. A Bordar was often one of the younger sons of Villeins who had a few acres of land and worked one day each week for the overlord. The Serfs were almost slaves and worked as servants. It was probable that the sheep would be pastured on the marshlands which lay to one side of what is now the area from Hall Lane towards the Marine Parade. Here the shepherds would milk the ewes and make cheeses in a shed called a "Wick". The system of what became known over the centuries as strip farms lasted in this country until well into the sixteenth century and in some areas until the nineteenth. There were no compact farms as we know them in this day and age. Strip farming meant that each man had strips of land scattered over three huge open fields which followed a simple system of crop rotation. The site of Dovercourt Green was once a common waste land on which the villagers were allowed to graze their animals. The sight of the war memorial marks the pound where stray animals were kept. It was not until the late thirteenth century that Harwich was becoming known of a place of some importance.

The estate of Dovercourt was handed over to the Earl of Norfolk. It was his son Roger who first united the District of Dovercourt with a small district which was to become known as Harwich.

1253 - Weekly market was granted to be held in Harwich.

1274 - Quarrel began with Ipswich over their trading ships being stopped at Harwich for tolls - and the practice of erecting fishing barriers across the river tides.

1294 - Harwich ordered to provide ships and men for Edward I - the battle against the Welsh.

1301 - Harwich ordered to provide ships and men for battle against the Scots.

1304 - Flemish weavers began landing at Harwich.

1318 - The King - Edward II - granted that a charter be given to the town of HARWICH so that it may become a Free Borough, with a market every week on Tuesday.

1326 - Landing of Queen Isabella and her lover Roger Mortimer.

1336 - Edward III - War with France. The English king protected the Flemmings in Flanders, his main market for wool.
The people of Flanders supported the King against the French.

1340 - Battle of SLUYS - made Harwich harbour important and brought business to the borough.

At the seige of Calais; Harwich provided 14 ships - 283 seamen.

Henry V re-opened hostilities.

Richard II (1377-99) granted tax-relief to rebuild the castle walls that was to the N/E of the town.

Export - mainly wool. Imports - wine, beans and cloth.

1514 - Henry VIII founded Trinity House.

1534 - Fortification built on Beacon Hill.

1543 - War broke out with Scotland and France. Henry VIII visits Harwich.

1551 - Town flooded.

1553 - JULY: Edward IV died in London.

1553 - Willerby left Harwich on an abortive attempt to seek the N/E passage.

1558 - Mary died. Elizabeth came to the throne of England.

1561 - Elizabeth visited Harwich and stayed in a house said to stand on the corner of Kings Head Street and St. Austins Lane.

1572 - Elizabeth starts secret run across the North Sea to help the Dutch fight the Spanish.

1574 - (JUNE 2) Duke of Norfolk executed on Tower Hill. Parish of Dovercourt and Harwich passed to the Crown.

1576 - Frobisher left on voyage of discovery for the N/W passage.

1585 - Seamen away fishing, only 20 men left to defend the town.

1597 - Queen Elizabeth I - transferred her rights to the Attorney General who granted a charter for the election of what today we know as a town council.

Plans of Harwich - 1500-1600

Harwich Harbour, as viewed from Beacon Hill

Original entrance of Old Harwich via the High Lighthouse

Voting return on Samuel Pepys as Member of Parliament for Harwich

1600 - Court of Common Council formed to run the town.

1604 - APRIL 18th - James I granted a new charter to the town of Harwich.
The village of Dovercourt and the Borough of Harwich were to form one common council.

1661 - After restoration of the monarchy the Postmaster General and the Dutch Ambassador agreed a new fast service between their respective countries. The boats carried passengers and thus began the paquet boat mail services.

1665 - Erection of lighthouse by Sir W. BATTEN.

1667 - Harwich ceased to be a naval station when the Royal Dockyard was opened in Sheerness.
Accession of William III - War with France followed - Warships again built at Harwich yards until death of Anne 1714.

1673 - Passenger ferry began from Harwich to Ipswich on each Sunday, it being market day in Ipswich.

1685 - Samuel Pepys and Anthony Deane elected as M.P.

1686 - William of Orange landed at Brixham.

1689 - William and Mary declared as joint rulers.

1691 - William went to Harwich en route for Holland.

1711 - 5 paquet boats to Holland.

1713 - Admiralty gave up Navyard.

1714 - Accession of George I - (A century of prosperity begins for Harwich)
Many fine houses in West Street and Church Street built - mainly due to the paquet boats - revised interests in the cod war - or perhaps because most of the time we were at war with France. During the second half of the century there was an attempt to put Dovercourt on the map as a spa watering-place. People were working and supported the House of Hanover.

1730 - There was five postal ships on the run from Harwich to Helvoetsluis. They were named the "Prince of Wales" the "Despatch" the "Eagle" the "Dolphin" and the "Duke of Marlborough" - on average they were only 53ft. long and 18½ft. wide.

1812 - New industry - making of Roman cement. The stone from Beacon Hill Cliff being broken up, burned in kilns, ground into powder, packed into 4 cwt kegs and sold in London for 7/6d. per cask.

1832 - Paquet Boat Mail service left Harwich for Tilbury.

1854 - August 15th - the official opening of Manningtree to Harwich Eastern Counties rail route.

1853 - Parliament authorised the building of a new quay face - and gas works and a railway station.

EXCURSIONS FROM HARWICH TO ROTTERDAM
THE FIRST RAIL-SEALINK JOURNEY

The article below is based on information printed in the 'Morning Herald', London 19th June 1846.

The directors of the Eastern Union Railway are desirous at as early a period as possible to develop the access of traffic which they anticipate travelling over their own line, in common with the Eastern Counties and Colchester line. It is planned when a regular communication with the continent can be established from Harwich harbour, to make an arrangement with the Orwell Steam Navigation Company to take their steam-vessel the Orwell, on an excursion trip from Ipswich and Harwich to Rotterdam and back, This will start from the former port, the railway not being yet completed to Harwich.

For many years the most energetic attempts have been made by influential gentlemen in the counties of Essex and Suffolk to recover for the ports of Harwich and Ipswich, (more especially for Harwich), a portion of that traffic with the coasts of Holland and London which it exclusively enjoyed for a long period, before the more general use of steam-vessels diverted the prosperity from Harwich. Now that the railway has brought those ports within two hours of the metropolis, and the eligibility of Harwich as a harbour of refuge and as a paquet station have been recently so conclusively established as to have induced the government to spend some money on its improvements, the directors of the newly formed Harwich Steam-paquet Company thought the present a most appropriate opportunity for showing what could really be effected.

Accordingly a special train left the London terminus at Shoreditch on Wednesday morning at half-past five o'clock, with some of the directors and other gentlemen invited to accompany them on the trip. It arrived at Ipswich, a distance of 68 miles, at 20 minutes past seven. Here, they were joined by some other gentlemen connected with the railways, and the party from the proposed Harwich Steam-paquet Company, and Mr. Miller, engineer, of Blackwall & Co. They proceeded directly on board the Orwell steamer, lying alongside the quay, and the signal for departure was given by firing a gun. They set off at 35 minutes to eight, at a rapid pace, down the picturesque river Orwell.

The sun shone most resplendently, and the morning gave promise of an agreeable and speedy passage across. The tide had ebbed for a quarter of an hour, and the little wind that was stirring was a gentle breeze from the ESE, which served rather to temper the power of the sun than to impede in any way the progress. The steamer had travelled 12 miles towards Harwich. It was at 8.20. The vessel lay to for a few minutes, and then continued her course. Leaving the government works of the Cliff Foot (rendered necessary for the purpose of narrowing the current and scouring the harbour), she passed the Altar Shoal and was off Landguard Fort on the opposite side at 8.30. The Orwell passed the Cork light-ship in a quarter of an hour from this time, the sea view extending and the breeze freshening - "rippling, but not roughening to a wave". In another hour she was off the north-east Shipwash light-vessel, the breeze, still strengthening, right in her teeth, with a little swell abreast Orfordness, the haze obscuring the land every minute on one side, the open sea ahead. Dotted here and there were a sail or two, and a tiny fleet of cement-stone dredging vessels with their single sails and irregular height of masts, forming an interesting spread on the horizon of the starboard bow. The land was soon lost sight of, and steering directly for the opposite coast, the Orwell met the tide off Shoen, about 20 miles from the Brill. It was four o'clock. The wind had considerably increased from the same quarter, whence it had blown during the passage. The swell had also grown. Hours had elapsed without a vessel of any kind being seen, when a solitary sail was sighted to windward. In a few minutes this became a Dutch pilot boat of box-like proportions. Speaking to her hardy navigator as the Orwell passed, she learned from him that she was about 12 miles off course, and her head was immediately turned in the proper direction. A few miles more steaming on the right track secured a pilot, who, seeing the signal flying, hove-to and came on board. Both vessel and skipper appeared the anti-type of the phantom ship, old Vanderdecken - the one well-adapted to keep the North Sea in any weather, and the other a fine, bold-looking, intelligent specimen of a seaman. He seemed rather astonished on hearing that the party had left London that morning and had put on another coat and pair of trousers securing the latter with a twist of rope-yarn round his waist. He visited the wheel and saw all was right, and then took his station on the paddle-box, having pronounced that the Orwell was "twelve" miles from the Brill. At 6.30 she reached it, and soon after entered the Maese. The visit of the Custom-house officials here caused at least an hour's delay, which was less tedious. However, an excellent dinner on deck occupied the attention of the company, at which "The Health of his Majesty the King of the Netherlands", "The Health of Queen Victoria", and "Perpetual Amity between Great Britain and Holland", were drunk.

The remainder of the passage up the Maese to Rotterdam was most delightful and enchanting, the setting sun shedding a gorgeous halo around every object on land and water. Rotterdam was at length reached at a quarter before nine, and the happy party was soon in comfortable shore quarters at the Grand Hotel des Pays Bas, having been only fifteen and a quarter hours from London, including stoppages of at least a couple of hours. Furthermore the steamer had proceeded all the way against a head wind, some swell, and for some time against the tide.

At half past ten yesterday morning the Orwell started, on her return passage. The day, if possible was still more glorious than the one preceding. With a "flowing sail", the gallant steamer was assisted across from Brill, and arrived at Ipswich, against tide, at half-past ten p.m., the party having again dined on board, and done honour to her Majesty, and the hero of the 18th of June. The healths of Mr. Cobbold, the Chairman, and the Directors of the enterprising Eastern Union Railway Company, who, in instituting the present experiment, had gone further than any other railway company, were toasted. Mr. Cobbold, in acknowledging the same, descanted on the success which had attended the trip, and on the ultimate mutual advantage to be derived by England and Holland, in the establishment of a line of steam ships, in connection with the railway for regular communication.

At 11 o'clock p.m. the special train started from Ipswich with the London residents and arrived in town at one this morning, the trip to Ipswich and Rotterdam, and from Rotterdam to Ipswich and London, having occupied only forty three and half hours. Of these thirteen and a quarter were spent on shore at Rotterdam; thus thirty and a quarter hours only, including all stoppages, were expended in the trip.

On the arrival of the Orwell at Rotterdam, Mr. Alfred Cobbold, one of the passengers, proceeded immediately to the Hague, and placed in the hands of his Majesty's ministers several copies of the 'Morning Herald', published in London on the morning of that day. That gentleman also forwarded copies of the 'Morning Herald' to Amsterdam, and to other parts of Holland. Strolling into a club house with the fact of his unprecedentedly rapid travelling having transpired by means of a copy of the 'Morning Herald', he was 'nen. con' elected an honorary member, and admitted to all the privileges of the institution.

The results of this experiment leave no doubt that when the railway is completed to Harwich and effective steamers are placed on the station between that port and Rotterdam, a traveller may leave London at six o'clock in the morning and arrive at the Hague, covering a distance of 234 miles, at six o'clock in the evening. Also letters from Holland will be able to reach London on the same day they are written in time for being posted to all parts of the world in the evening. The Orwell performed the passage in very quick time, considering that she is only of 80 horse power to 230 tons. She is one of the first iron boats built in the river by Ditchburn and Mare, and it speaks very highly for the engineers, Messrs. Miller, Ravenhill and Co., of Blackwall, that although for seven years, her beam-engines, which were pronounced by Professor Fary to be the most perfect ever fitted, have been at constant work. The Orwell ran the distance of 154 statute miles, including stoppages in 19 hours, working only at about 14lbs. pressure. With more modern-built boats, however, of greater horse power in proportion to tonnage, and working at a similar pressure as the new Dover boats, the distance could be performed in a shorter space, and the passage from London to Rotterdam could be made in perhaps less than half the time than that now occupied by the steam-boats which run from the Thames and carry the mails.

The 'Rotterdam Courant', yesterday, announced in its columns the extraordinary feat of railway and steam-ship travelling, it quoted from the 'Morning Herald' of Wednesday, containing full reports of the debates in parliament, which did not close until that morning, having reached there the same evening in time for publication.

1854 - North of Europe service to Antwerp p.s. AQUILA (300 tons) only on service for a few months.

1855 - April 12th - CYGNUS and AQUILA chartered by E.C. Railways for Antwerp Service. 3 Sailing per week from October and weekly services by AQUILA only December 12th - services discontinued.

1862 - GER Co., formed and took control of the E.C. London - Harwich route.

1863 - Weekly services ran by G.E.R. to Rotterdam. GPO Mails return via Harwich for Holland.
G.E.C. Railway planning moves to expand the port of Harwich.

28/3/1863 - GER directors visit Harwich with plan to commence continental service.

24/7/1863 - GER (Steam Boats) Bill - has third reading and passed.

28/7/1863 - GER (Steam Boats) Bill - receives Royal assent.

11/9/1863 - Range of cattle sheds being erected on the new quay.

24/9/1863 - P.S. Blenheim, hired (3 months) from Todd, McGregor of Glasgow at £170 per week inc. insurance and part crew charges.
640 gross tons: 320 nett: 350 NHP - For twice weekly service.

3/10/1863 - BLENHEIM starts service - Rotterdam 1430: Harwich 4/10 (0800) cattle in London by 1300.

28/10/1863 - Some of the crew deserted.

28/10/1863 - P.S. Norfolk - hired from Cuncliff & Watson of Goole. At £300 per month inc. crew and stores.

6/11/1863 - NORFOLK on service.

11/11/1863 - Blenheim charter extended until January 1864.

16/12/1863 - Prince of Wales chartered for 3 months at £70 per week.

1864 - Weekly service by G.E.R. to Antwerp. Service operated by the p.s. AVALON and p.s. ZEALOUS. Journey for the 120 miles sea crossing taking about 10 hours.

HARWICH DOCK & PIER COMPANY

Submitted plans in 1860 for the reclamation of land and the formation of a dock, tidal basin and pier, across the waters, which are now known as Bathside.

Plans submitted by the engineer, Peter Bruff, gave details of a new frontage - which is today the Quay of Harwich and concerning the erection of the new Continental Pier. This heralded the coming of the Eastern Counties Railway, with a line extending out into the harbour over a pier; which today in a shortened version is known as Trinity Pier.

If these plans had been followed through, the harbour would to this day have a tidal basin across the Train Ferry Terminal, leading through a lock. Ships would then be able to berth in a floating dock covering an area reaching to Parkeston Quay.

1860

The GER planned to expand eastward down the River Stour from Parkeston Quay and sought planning permission intending to reclaim land in the Bathside and erect a Graving Dock, with an entrance to the westward side of the then GER new pier.

At a later date it was planned to erect a break-water for a distance of one mile deviating from a point east of Dovercourt Dock River. This break-water would have carried a road and railway for a secondary pier to serve the continent steam-boat service.

Before long Parkeston Quay was fully operative, with its marshelling yard and workshops to the east of the station quay. Inside this area it was planned to erect a dry dock with an entrance through the sea wall or embankment.

Whilst shipping activities of Harwich Quay became limited to fishing boats and sundry craft, those of Parkeston, by the Parish of Ramsey, went full steam ahead.

19/1/1864 - Other ships chartered:-
p.s. PRIDE OF ERIN
p.s. PRINCESS ALICE at £80 per week.
p.s. KILLARNEY at £115 per week for 3 months.

30/3/1864 - Princess Alice charter renewed for 6 months at £101/10/- per week.

MAR/APL 1864 - "Rotterdam" and "Harwich" altered to accommodate passengers - 50 berths.

30/7/1864 - Antwerp service commenced.

30/9/1864 - New Railway Pier at Harwich now in use.

1/1/1865 - 20/10/1865 - Imported 145,007 cattle, sheep and pigs.

19/6/1867 - Decided to register ships at Harwich.

18/9/1867 - Letter of complaint and passengers on ROTTERDAM re Harwich/ Antwerp service. First of a variety to be received.

2/3/1868 - "GT. YARMOUTH" chartered to go to the Med., and Black Sea for commercial trading - sailed 7/3/1868 until 6/10/1869.

APRIL 1872 - Introduction of uniform for Captain, 1st and 2nd Officers: 1, 2 and 3 Stewards.

AUGUST 1872 - Belgian coal tested, but proved too expensive.

23/9/1873 - Examine possibility of using Flushing.

OCTOBER 1874 - Daily services to Antwerp and Rotterdam to offset GSN.

20/10/1846 - The Harwich Steam-packet Co., to be formed and financed by the Eastern Counties Railways - but were restrained by writ of shareholders.

30/3/1849 - Reported E.C.R. had purchased 6 ex- Government steamers for £35,000 for Harwich, Holland, Cuxhaven mails.

13/4/1849 - Scheme fell through, as railway unable to raise sufficient finance.

23/4/1855 - CYGNUS) Arrived at Harwich - chartered by E.C. Railways for

25/4/1855 - AQUILA) Antwerp Service.

2/5/1855 - 2 Sailings a week - until 20/10/1855.

20/10/1855 - Weekly service by AQUILA

12/12/1855 - Service discontinued.

4/6/1858 - Began new attempts by the E.C. Railway at Harwich/Continental service E.C. Railway and the Dutch Rhenish Union Transit Co.

1875 - p.s. CLAUD HAMILTON launched.

p.s. Claud Hamilton and p.s. Prince of Wales provided daily services to Rotterdam.

14/1/1879 - Contract to erect P/Q to Morseley Foundry Co., for £67,971/9/1d., and sheds to cost £9,500.

1880 - Danish service from Esberg to Harwich quay. p.s. RIBERHUSS lands cattle on June 4th.
Construction commenced on erecting quay on Ray Island (now Parkeston Quay).

p.s. RIBERHUSS - First Danish vessel to operate the service ESBJERG/HARWICH. First ship to discharge cargo at Parkeston Quay.

1882 - September 22nd p.s. RIBERHUSS arrives with first cargo of cattle to unload at Parkeston Quay.

1883 - February 14th
March 15th - Parkeston Quay officially opened.

1884 - August 19th Hamburg traffic commenced with weekly sailings of Astronome.

1886 -   s.s. COLCHESTER - joins the service to Rotterdam.
20/17/1887 - Only "HARWICH" on the cargo service - more trade going on Flushing
             route - Plan to charter cargo steamers:
             "CORSICAN" (338 tons) - 3 months at £300 per month.
8/12/1888 - "JOHN O'GROATS" - 3 months at £400 per month.

THE GREAT EASTERN RAILWAY COMPANY'S HARWICH FLEET

The advantage of communication with the continent from London are not wholly on the side of the lines which include the short sea routes, even when the South of Europe has to be visted by the traveller. For instance, the water being deep. larger boats can be put on between Harwich and Antwerp, and supposing the voyager to be sea-sick, he is not obliged to turn out of the boat when the attack is as its worst, and to join the train when he can scarcely walk; nor has he, while in this condition, to be packed upright with other persons in a compartment of a railway carriage. Between Harwich and Antwerp he can obtain the most part of a night's rest in a comfortable cabin, illuminated by electric light, and has time to recover from sea-sickness during the smooth passage of five hours up the river Scheldt to Antwerp. If he is not sea-sick he has advantages equal to that of a comfortable night's hotel accommodation, and in the morning finds that considerable part of the journey to Switzerland and Italy has been thus traversed.

A great alleviation of sea-sickness is due to the fact that two of the boats of the Great Eastern Railway Company are twin-screw ships, so that instead of the best part of the boat being allotted to the engines as in paddle steamers, this part falls to the lot of the first-class passengers. A ship when pitching resembles a see-saw, in which the amplitude of rise and fall is infinitely less at the centre than at the two ends, hence the advantage of removing engines, which are not sea-sick, from the best part of the boat. Tourists will find that communication between Antwerp and Italy and between Italy and Switzerland is expeditious and not very expensive. The fares on Belgian railways are much lower than in England and France for the same distances. In France, railway communication generally is dear and slow for all but first-class passengers, the trains being almost always so arranged that second-class passengers can only travel long distances at snail's pace unless they possess through tickets from England. The French railways are worked far more in the interests of the shareholders than in that of the public. In time, when their leases are out, they will all fall into the hands of the government and add enormously to its revenue, a fact which is usually overlooked by the newspapers when they speak of the present annual income and expenditure of France.

A plan to establish railway communication between London and the Eastern counties of England was projected in 1831, under the name of the London and Essex Railway, but it fell through. In 1834 the Eastern Counties Railway Company issued its prospectus, and in spite of opposition this company held its ground. It said:- "The benefits which will result from the Eastern Counties Railway will not become merely local and national; it will become the great highway to the British metropolis from Scotland, Holland, Germany, Hamburg and Lubeck, combining, with a happy union, public with private interests". The construction of the railway was commenced, but some of the share-holders lost heart when the shares were at 50 per cent discount; they were, in 1839, complelled by law to pay up, out of justice to other shareholders who had kept their engagements, and also to prevent the stoppage of the works. The result was that in 1839 the first train ran to Brentwood. The line was opened to Harwich on the 15th August, 1854, and that branch was constructed by a separate company.

Attention may now be turned to the existing Harwich steam fleet, the oldest portion of which, however, rarely sees active service.

THE AVALON, NEW STEAM-BOAT OF THE HARWICH AND ROTTERDAM LINE

The first of a fleet of steam-boats, which Messrs. Dudgeon, of Cubitt Town, Blackwall, are building for the Great Eastern Railway Company, to convey their traffic between the ports of Harwich and Rotterdam, is the Avalon. Her trial-trip, which took place on Saturday, the 21st May, 1864, was a decided success. Above 150 gentlemen were present, amongst whom were the chairman, deputy-chairman, and directors of the Great Eastern Railway, several of the more prominent proprietors, the Mayors of Yarmouth, Ipswich, Lynn, Wisbeach, Maldon and Harwich, and a number of merchants, agriculturists, and others interested in trade, foreign cattle and steam navigation. The party went down by a special train from Bishopsgate station to Tilbury, where they embarked on board the Avalon and proceeded down the river to witness her performances at "the measured mile". This proof was most satisfactory, as she attained a speed of fourteen knots, or seventeen statute miles an hour. She is a paddle-wheel steamer, with no particular novelty in her construction or machinery; but she is remarkable for some of her internal fittings, which display much originality of design. It should be observed that she is built for mails, passengers, and their personal luggage only. For all live stock between Harwich and Rotterdam there are cattle-boats; and as the passenger-boats carry no cattle, so the cattle-boats carry no passengers.

Instead of the bridge of ordinary steamers, the Avalon is provided with a hurricane deck capacious enough to accommodate 150 persons. It is, as near as can be, one third of the entire length of the ship. At the after end of the hurricane deck a short bridge spans the short open space of the deck where the passengers come on board; and crossing the short bridge, we are on the poop. This is somewhat larger than the hurricane deck, and is, makes, a glorious promenade. A flight of easy steps on the port and starboard sides leads down to the open space of the deck. To the right and left of the saloon entrance are approaches to the berths, which are most conveniently arranged. The dimensions of the Avalon are:- 245ft over all, 230ft on the water-line, 27ft wide, 12.8ft dept of hold. The engines are oscillating, of 200 horse-power, nominal, and capable of working separately in case of a break down. Messrs. Dudgeon are the makers both of the ship and its engines.

OTHER SHIPS

The Zealous was built in 1864, of iron, by Messrs. Dudgeon and Co., of London. Her length is 230ft; width 27ft; tonnage 613; horse-power 950. It is licensed to carry 301 passengers. She was originally built for passengers only, and afterwards converted into a passenger-cargo ship. She steams 12 knots an hour. She ran on a tidal service to Rotterdam, and is now nearly worn out.

The Harwich was built in 1864 by Messrs. Simpson and Co., of London, for the cattle trade between Harwich and Antwerp. Her length is 215ft; width 27ft; tonnage 1000; horse-power 980; speed 12 knots an hour. Subsequently she was converted into a passenger and cargo boat, and licensed to carry 110 passengers. The accommodation being too small she was again converted into a cargo boat, fitted with twin screws.

The Rotterdam, also built in 1864, is a sister ship to the Harwich, her tonnage, however, is 757; horse-power 1060. Subsequently she was converted from a cattle into a cargo and passenger boat, to carry 108 passengers. Then she was used as a relief boat, running on the winter service when required. That is to say, when some of the larger boats were under repairs, and the passengers were few. She was only used in case of emergency, as there were two other spare boats.

The Pacific, built in 1864, by Langley, of London, is 235ft long, 26ft wide, 712 tonnage, 700 horse-power, and carries 400 passengers. She was not built specially for the Great Eastern Railway Company, which lengthened her 30ft after the purchase. She was laid up because she steams at only 10 knots an hour, and is too slow for the passenger service.

The Avalon, built by Dudgeon in 1865, is 239ft long, 27ft wide, 670 tonnage, 1000 horse-power, and carries 483 passengers. She was constructed to carry passengers, cattle and cargo for the Rotterdam trade. She has been fitted with new boilers, and her engines have been altered from common jet. Her speed is 12 knots an hour. She does not run regularly, but is put on occasionally to relieve other vessels.

The Richard Young, built in 1871, by Dudgeon, is a sister ship to the Avalon; her tonnage is 718, horse-power 950, and she carries 607 passengers. She steams 12 knots an hour, and is only used occasionally to relieve other vessels.

The Claud Hamilton was built in 1875 by Messrs. J. Elder and Co., Glasgow; her length is 251ft; width 30ft; tonnage 962; horse-power 1596; and carries 558 passengers. She carries passengers and cargo, has combined oscillating engines, and steams 13 knots an hour. She ran regularly between Harwich and Rotterdam.

The Prince of Wales was built in 1878 by the London and Glasgow Shipbuilding Company. Her length is 265ft; width 30ft; tonnage 1098; horse-power 1800; number of passengers 579. She has surface-condensing engines, not compound, steams 14 knots and hour, and carries passengers and cargo. She is usually running to Antwerp.

The Lady Tyler was built in 1880 by Messrs. T. & W. Smith, North Shields. Her length is 261ft; width 30ft; tonnage 995; horse-power 1700, and carries 709 passengers. She has compound surface-condensing steeple engines, with six cylinders, two of them high-pressure, and the other four low-pressure. She is specially built to carry much weight whilst drawing little water, and although only built as a twelve and a half knot boat, she steams 13 knots regularly.

The Adelaide was built in 1880 by the Barrow Shipbuilding Company. Her length is 254ft; width 32ft; tonnage 968; horse-power 2000; passengers 705. She is a paddle boat, built of steel, with compound oscillating engines. Her engines are largely constructed of steel, and she runs regularly in the Rotterdam trade. She steams fourteen and a half knots, and carries much weight with small draught of water. To reach Rotterdam in all states of tide, it is necessary that the boats should not draw more than 10ft or 11ft of water.

We come now to the two new twin-screw boats, the Norwich and Ipswich, built in 1883 by Earles' Shipbuilding Company, at Hull. These were the first two ferries to sail from Parkeston. They are 260ft in length; 31ft wide; 1060 tonnage; 2000 horse-power; carry 440 passengers and steam fourteen and a half knots an hour. Their hulls, shafting, a propellers are of steel. They were specially built for the service between Harwich and Antwerp, and draw 15ft of water. The saloons are amidships; the second-class accommodation is aft. They are provided with water-balance tanks capable of holding 200 tons of water for trimming the ship when the cargo is light, but as they are substantial heavy ships, these tanks are not of much use, and they will probably be broken into a gain space for other purposes. On the main deck are fittings for carrying horses fore and aft the saloon, which is formed by a long bridge amidship. The entrance to the saloon is through the deck house on the bridge. The deck house os ultised partly for private cabins, and partly for steering gear; there is a look-out for the officers on the top. The panels in the saloon are of rose-wood, satin-wood and oak. The ship is heated by steam, fitted with electric bells, and illuminated by Swan's incandescent electric lights, of which one is kept in action all night in every cabin. The Siemen's dynamos are in the engine room. They are driven by a special engine. The electrical arrangements are by Raworth of Liverpool. Great care has been taken to secure efficient ventilation. Upcast and downcast ventilators are fitted for the saloons and sleeping cabins. These admit fresh air so effectually that the passengers often plug the ventilators to keep it out. There is a smoking-room between the cabin and the poop. The galley is situated on the main

s.s. J.C. LACOUR

s.s. A.P. BERNSTOFF

s.s. AVALON

deck between the engine and boiler space, with a hoist leading up to the bridge to enable the stewards to pass the dishes to the cabin without going upon the main deck. This is found to be a very convenient arrangement.

These two vessels were designed by Mr. W.G. Ramsden of Liverpool, and backed by Captain Howard, the Great Eastern Railway Company's marine superintendent at Harwich, whose long experience there made him well acquainted with the requirements of that special service. Some say that these twin-screw boats roll a little more than paddle steamers; others say that they do not. The vessels have each two pairs of compound surface-condensing engines; the high-pressure cylinders are 30 inches in diameter, and the low-pressure 57 inches, with a 36 inch stroke; they were made by Earle's, and run with a piston speed of 550ft per minute, under a working pressure of 80 lb. The steel shafting is 10 inches in diameter; the propeller boss and blades are of steel; there are four blades on each. The vessels have each two of Blake's donkey engines, with 6 inch pumps, for discharging water ballast and bilges, filling closets and tanks, and so on. A Blake's 5 inch pump is used in washing the decks. The engines are fitted with Brown's hydraulic starting gear, and are so arranged that one man can start both pairs of engines. The two double-ended boilers are 18ft 6 in long, with three furnaces at each end. These boilers are of the "best" Staffordshire iron, nine sixteenths of an inch thick. The vessels have each three hatchways, three steam winches and derricks for discharging cargo. They are fitted with Bow and McLauchlan's steering gear, also with Napier's steam windlasses. Each ship carries five boats, one of William's seat rafts, and one of Copeman's life-buoy seats. In fact they are excellent vessels altogether, giving much satisfaction to their owners and to the passengers.

1893 - Hook of Holland sea depot opened.
s.s. CHELMSFORD joined service to Holland.
1894 - 28,677 tons of Danish bacon imported.
1895 - s.s. AMSTERDAM (1), BERLIN and VIENNA ordered.
1896 - p.s. ADELAIDE - last of the paddle steamers sold.
1897 - s.s. DRESDEN - ordered.
1901 - October 1st - "J.C. LACOUR" - first purpose built passenger ship arrives on her Esbjerg maiden journey.
1902 - s.s. BRUSSELS - first vessel fitted with sea/shore radio to assist Marconi with experiment.
1903 - June 1st - The service between Parkeston and the Hook of Holland commenced today.
21/11/1905 - G.E.R. (Steamboats) Act 1904; grants powers to sail into Zeebrugge, so that Zeebrugge can be used instead of Ostend (last used 1895) when Antwerp becomes ice-bound.
27/10/1908 - Yarmouth (Capt. A.J. Aris) left Rotterdam 0504 - 354 tons cargo, 89 tons meat - (Hook with 443 tons cargo and 192 tons meat) and 3 x 3 ton furniture vans.
One body recovered by H.M.S. BLAKE.
Enquiry 1/1/1909: Companies liability £6,024 - "Ship in unseaworthy condition.
1910 - Booking at Parkeston Quay: Rail trucks drawn from sidings to east end of quay. Coal tipped into barges then towed to ships, coaled by hand.
Cost £4,200 per annum. Tipper suggested with conveyors to berth and loading shoot.
May 7th - s.s. BALDER opens service to Gothenburg.
1913 - a.p. BERNSTOFF arrives on maiden voyage for Esbjerg.
October - DR. RUDOLF DIESEL, - inventor the worlds renowned engine - disappears from s.s. DRESDEN - bound for Parkeston Quay.

1914 - August 4th - Railway services transferred to Tilbury for duration of World War I.
        August 6th - Hook services suspended.
        August 13th - Esbjerg service transferred to Leith.
        October 4th - Antwerp service suspended.
        October 5th - Rotterdam service suspended - Resumed weekly for Tilbury.

1916 - June 22nd - s.s. BRUSSELS - Captured by Germans.

1917 - March 21st - s.s. COPENHAGEN torpedoed.

1918 - November 11th - Armistice Day.

26/11/1918 - "Quentin" - (Gibson & Co., Leith)   On Rotterdam Service.
             "Glasgow" - (Rankin Line, Glasgow)

6/2/1919 -   Parkeston Quay/Antwerp service resumed using:-
             "WOODCOCK" and "MARYLEBONE" - (twice weekly)

6/3/1919 -   Parkeston Quay/Rotterdam service resumed using:-
             "STAVELEY" and "NOTTS" - (twice weekly).
             Parkeston Quay, Rotterdam and Antwerp relief ships - "PRINCESS
             IRMA" and the "CROMER".

17/6/1919 - "Princess Irma" returned to owners - "Princess Beatrice" on Antwerp
             service and April 1920.

26/6/1919 - "St. George" - purchased from the Canadian Pacific Railways for Hook
             service.

6/11/1919 - Kilkenny returned to Parkeston Quay - renamed Frinton.

8/8/1919 -   Notts returned to G.C.R.

1920 -   Investigation into inauguarating a Harwich/Calais service - started
             2/9/1920 stopped due to lack of service.

12/4/1923 - LNER - retain GER houseflag.

3-8/7/1926 - General strike at Antwerp, traffic diverted to Zeebrugge.

1/1/1927 -   Zeeland to operate at Parkeston Quay.

26/8/1928 - Antwerp
             Bruges   supplied with gramophones.
             Maline

T.S.S. NORWICH
Launched 24th October, 1883, sister ship to the "IPSWICH", was given a new boiler in 1897; and served until 1912 when she was sold to new owners in Turkey.

P.S. CLAUD HAMILTON
John Elder launched this ship on the 3rd June, 1875; and she was the largest steamer the company had placed on their continental service to that date. She took her name from the then chairman of the company. She served the company for 22 years and must be given credit for a great deal of the popularity given to the Harwich-Hook service. in 1898 she was sold to the Corporation of the City of London. Dutch shipbreakers purchased her in July 1914 for dismantling.

P.S. RAVENSBURY
A sister ship to the "AVALON" (II) and employed on the Harwich-Rotterdam service. She sprung a leak and was abandoned at the river entrance to Rotterdam on the 18th March, 1870, becoming the first loss to the Railway's Harwich fleet. Her wreck was discovered in November 1971. Dredging crew operating in the Maasvlakte lifted half the vessel exposing the square steamboilers, two oscillating engines and paddle with wooden blades. Wreck was reburied in its muddy grave.

T.S.S. CAMBRIDGE
Built in 1886, launched 11th October, 1886, she served on the Rotterdam, Hook and Antwerp services, before being sold on 25th November 1912. Was in collision with H.M.S. SALMON (12th December 1911). Two of the destroyer's crew were killed, the remainder being rescued.

P.S. PRINCESS OF WALES
Launched 2nd February, 1878, a two masted paddle steamer which operated from Harwich to Rotterdam and from Parkeston to the Hook. Sold for scrap 16th May 1895.

On a historical note it is interesting to relate that the then Princess of Wales, was formerly Alexandra, Princess of Denmark; sister of King Frederik VIII of Denmark who was the Great Grandfather to Queen Margrethe II: she married the Prince of Wales, later Edward VII, King of Great Britain, Great Grandfather to our present Queen, Elizabeth II.

T.S.S. CHELMSFORD
Launched 21st February 1893, had the distinction of being the vessel to open the Harwich-Hook service. Was disposed of by sale to the Great Western Railway, who renamed her "BRETONNE" in June 1910.

P.S. RICHARD YOUNG S.S. BRANDON
This steamer was commissioned by the G.E.R. at a time when their Harwich-Holland service was becoming established. Its arrival for service likewise coincided with the improvements made by the Dutch in creating a New Waterway into Rotterdam. (This Waterway must in no way be confused with the Terminal at the Hook). Thus, this vessel had the distinction, that on her maiden voyage to Holland, she was the first ship to sail through the new Waterway. In 1890 she was converted to a screw ship and until she was sold to the Dutch in 1905 for scrapping, was known as the S.S. BRANDON.

T.S.S. COLCHESTER (I)
Commissioned in 1889, she had a long career as a merchant vessel, until she was captured by the Germans during the 1914-18 war and subsequently sunk by the Royal Navy.

T.S.S. ST. PETERSBURG ARCHANGEL
Sister ship of the "COPENHAGEN" and "MUNICH", one of the first turbine steamers on the Harwich service, but the last of the three to come onto the route. She was renamed the "ARCHANGEL" in 1919. Whilst acting as a troop carrier during the 1939-45 war, she was bombed and sunk on 16th May, 1941.

T.S.S. COPENHAGEN
A sister ship to the "MUNICH" and "ST. PETERSBURG", she became the first turbine steamer on the Harwich route and had accommodation for two classes of passengers. Sunk by torpedo on 21st March, 1917.

T.S.S. MUNICH
Sister ship to the "COPENHAGEN" and "ST. PETERSBURG" and with these two helped to make the Harwich-Hook service an established route to the continent in the pre 1914-18 war era. Renamed "ST. DENIS" in 1916, she served during this war as a hospital ship, and retained the name "ST. DENIS" when she reverted to her peace time role of a passenger ship.

After being scuttled in Rotterdam (May 1940) she was raised and used by the German Navy. She returned into British hands in 1945.

Was used for temporary housing by the Civic Authorities in Germany before being returned to Britain in 1950 for scrapping.

1910 - Idyllic scenes of Edwardian Harwich harbour

T.S.S. AMSTERDAM (I)
One of three sister ships which came into the service in 1894. She lasted until December 1928. Her sister ships were "BERLIN" and "VIENNA" (I).

T.S.S. VIENNA (I) ROULERS
Launched 18th July, 1894, a sister ship to the "AMSTERDAM" (I) and "BERLIN", she was in service in 1894. She was renamed "ROULERS" in 1920 being employed on the Harwich-Zeebrugge service, before being scrapped in March 1930.

S.S. BERLIN - Breaking up by the rough tides - across the mole at the entrance to Hook of Holland.

T.S.S. BERLIN
Sister ship to the "AMSTERDAM" (I) and "VIENNA". Was wrecked at the entrance to the River Maas, with a great loss of life on 21st February, 1907.

T.S.S. BRUSSELS
One of the few rail ships not requisitioned during the 1914-18 war. Used by the Germans after her capture on the 22nd June, 1916. Scuttled at the entrance to Zeebrugge harbour 14th October, 1917. Was raised after the war to finish her career as "LADY BRUSSELS" off the west coast after being sold by the G.E.R. in 1920. Broken up in 1929.

S.S. GREAT YARMOUTH
Built in London 1866, but as her passenger accommodation was insufficient she was sold in 1872. Was chartered for 3 months in 1876 by G.E.R. to cover a ship shortage. Used in the coal trade from Gateshead, 1881, she was stranded in the Gulf of Bothnia September 1887 and became a total wreck.

T.S.S. NEWMARKET
Served as a cargo vessel from August 1907. Lost on war service 16th July 1916.

T.S.S. CLACTON
Sister ship to the "NEWMARKET" and used as a cargo vessel. Lost on war service on 22nd October, 1917.

T.S.S. BRUGES
Sister ship to the "ANTWERP". Destroyed by enemy action off the French coast 26th June, 1940.

T.S.S. ANTWERP
One of two (the other being the "BRUGES") first class ships built for the Harwich-Antwerp service. Sold in April 1950 for scrap.

T.S.S. DRESDEN
Launched 4th November, 1896, came into service 1897; was re-named "LOUVAIN" in 1915 and was lost on war service 20th January 1918.

T.S.S. YARMOUTH
Sister ship to the "CROMER" she came into service in 1903 as a cargo ship. Was last seen on the night of 27th October, 1908, when she became one of the unsolved mysteries of the sea.

T.S.S. CROMER
Was utilised on the service as a cargo ship, along with her sister ship the "YARMOUTH". After 32 years service was scrapped in 1934.

T.S.S. STOCKHOLM
This twin-screw vessel was under construction in the yards of John Brown's at Clydebank, and was intended to be named as above, but she became the rail ship that never was, because, she was converted during the 1914-18 war into an aircraft carrier, serving the Royal Navy as H.M.S. PEGASUS. Broken up 1931.

T.S.S. ST. GEORGE (I)
She was built by Cammeil Laird for the Fisherguard-Rosslare route in 1906. She appears to have been the property of the Canadian Pacific Railway since 1913 and acquired by the G.E.R. in 1919. In October 1929 she was sold and scrapped in Blyth.

S.S. KILKENNY
One of the few importations into the Railway's fleet. She was built in 1903 being on the Liverpool-Dublin run for the City of Dublin S.P. Co., Liverpool. The G.E.R. purchased her in 1917, renaming her "FRINTON" in 1919. She was retained 10 years in the Harwich fleet before being sold to Greek owners, 29th July 1926.

1924 - April 24th - Commencement of Train Ferry to Zeebrugge.
1925 - August 8th - m.s. PARKESTON arrives on Maiden voyage.
1926 - June 28th - m.s. JYLLAND arrives on maiden voyage.
        September 16th - m.s. SHERINGHAM (LNER Cargo boat) arrives alongside Parkeston Quay.
1927 - January 1st - Stoomuart Matschappis Zeeland commences connection with the FLUSHING route.

m.s. ORANGE NASSAU - first S.M.Z. vessel to sail from Parkeston Quay.

1929 - April 26th - s.s. ESBJERG arrives on her maiden voyage.
July 8th - s.s. VIENNA (2) arrives at Parkeston Quay to commence her service.

1930 - February 22nd - s.s. PRAGUE - first ship fitted with duty free shop, arrives at Parkeston for Hook service.
April 26th - s.s. AMSTERDAM (2) made maiden voyage to the Hook.

1934 - August 30th - s.s. CROMER - left for brakers yard.

1938 - s.s. VIENNA made first cruise.

One of the original TRAIN FERRY Steamers.

"BACON BOAT" - alongside Parkeston Quay.

1950 - Unloading bacon by hand.

1970 - Unloading bacon. RO/RO refrigerator van. Bacon introduced from pork-form to seller.

M.S. PARKESTON

M.S. ESBJERG

QUEEN OF CRUISING

The eighth and last weekend cruise of a highly successful season terminated with the return of the 'Vienna' on Monday, September the 19th, 1928, to Harwich (Parkeston Quay). Apart from a wonderfully fine and sunny weekend, a goodly company on board, sumptuous food (as usual), and a positive galaxy of pleasure, there was a novel item on the programme in the crowning of Cruisiana, North Sea Queen.

On Saturday, each and every woman on board wore a numbered ticket, whilst the sterner sex, remembering that the ballot was secret, gazed enigmatically at the bevy around him. To echo Dell Leigh - "Is there any neater sight than an English woman in a cardigan suit and beret?" No! To cut a long and very interesting story short, the votes were counted at 11.30 p.m. on Saturday and at eight bells precisely, Miss Brenda Clapin, of Tonbridge, was announced as having been elected by her fellow passengers as Cruisiana, North Sea Queen.

As the 'Vienna' steamed down the Scheldt on Sunday morning, the coronation was held with due pomp and ceremony on deck, the Queen being attended by two pages, Miss E. Moones, of Reddish, Stockport, and Miss R. Whitmore, of Dovercourt, runners-up in order of popularity. Captain Booth, master of the 'Vienna', amidst a fanfare of trumpets, received the Queen in the traditional gallant manner of the Merchant Service, saying:-

> Hail! gracious, chosen North Sea Queen!
> Thy loyal Subjects here are seen
> Assembled all around thee.
> Accept our homage dutiful
> O Cruisiana beautiful,
> May joys for e'er surround thee!
> Hail sovereign, who beloved of every Tar is -
> Cruisiana, Regina Maris!

He then proceeded to crown the Queen, who handed a manuscript to the Prime Minister. Mr. S. Vernon Harcourt (the "Premier") bowed to the company and read Her Majesty's speech, as follows (I may say that this speech is from the pen of our well-known contributor, Julian Kaye):-

> My heartfelt thanks to you my lieges gay
> For having crowned me as your Queen today,
> No monarch craved for subjects better than
> This happy, joyous, peaceful little clan;
> It is, indeed, a joy to be a Queen.
> 'Twill be remembered many years I ween.
>
> This fleeting summer, now alas! nigh spent,
> Has seen this ship of mine on pleasure bent.
> Across my seas she's carried jocund folk
> To fill the summer night with dance and joke.
> They left their daily cares and toils in town
> And came away all thoughts of work to drown.
> At sea they found they were indeed at home
> And at their will they could my good ship roam.
> Their every want I think they found supplied,
> And all their hosts to do their bidding vied.

And when in foreign parts they went ashore.
They found a kindly aegis to the fore.
So well and truly shepherded were they
That at each place they spent a day,
And breathed the freedom of the seaside air
That gave them zest to enjoy the ship's good fare.

This is the final cruise, now drops the curtain,
A duty falls upon your Queen I'm certain
To voice your thanks to all who've worked their best
To serve our ends and minister with zest.
Were I to name them all 'twould take an age
And tax the powers of a Queen more sage;
But I've an order meet for good and brave,
The "Royal Order of the Crested Wave".
And this should glisten on the manly breast
Of one who's given of his very best -
Our captain, to whose seamanship is due
The constant safety that's attended you.
Once more thanks, our love and or regard.
Step forward gallant Sir, "The accolade".
(She gives the accolade)

Her Majesty then uttered these words:-

Arise, Sir Captain; now you're Knighted!
With this ovation we're delighted,
Our thanks to all of you.

The Captain replied:-

Good Queen, my thanks, a man cannot say more.
I'll think most sweetly of you when ashore.

And so concluded a charming and novel ceremony which delighted not merely the passengers and chief actors of the pageant, but was an object of great interest to the occupants of the Dutch tug 'Raymond', which came alongside to gaze on the proceedings. Long live Queen Cruisiana, Queen of Cruising.

T.S.S. VIENNA (II)
Sister ship to the "PRAGUE" and "AMSTERDAM" (II). She was largely employed on weekend summer cruises. Was transferred to the Ministry of War Transport during the 1939-45 war, and under L.N.E.R. management was used as a troop carrier. At the end of hostilities she was used as a forces leave ship. She was disposed of in 1960 for breaking up.

S.S. VIENNA - as a cruise ship ...   *... as a troop ship*

M.S. KONINGIN EMMA

RO/RO pre-war 1938 view of car boarding the S.S. KONINGIN EMMA

Troop ship M.V. EMPIRE WANSBECK

T.S.S. AMSTERDAM (II)
Built in the 1930's with her sister ships "VIENNA" and the "PRAGUE". These were the first ships of which record can be found of having shops on board. Destroyed by enemy action off the coast of Normandy, August 1944.

S.S. MECKLENBURG - pre-war

S.S. FELIXSTOWE

Built in 1918 by Hawthorns of Leith, launched 11th May, 1918, she served more or less as a tramp steamer until 1942, when requisitioned by the Admiralty she served as H.M.S. COLCHESTER. Reverting to her peace time role and named as S.S. FELIXSTOWE in September 1946. In the summer of 1948 she was on the Weymouth-Channel Islands route. She was sold 18th October 1950 to the Limerick Steamship Company Limited and renamed "KYLEMORE". She was broken up at Rotterdam towards the end of 1957.

S.S. PRINSES JULIANA

T.S.S. MALINES
Built in 1921, she was the last vessel acquired by the G.E.R. before the Harwich fleet was absorbed into the L.N.E.R. The upper portion of the fore part of the ship, like those of the "ANTWERP" and "BRUGES" was painted white. After a varied peace and wartime career she was sunk off Port Said in 1942. When raised she became the property of the Ministry of War Transport, being managed by the General Steam Navigation Company. Sold for scrapping in 1948.

1939 -	June 4th -	m.s. KONINGIN EMMA arrives to fit into services to Flushing. m.s. PRINCESS BEATRIX arrives to fit into services to Flushing.
	September 3rd -	War declared. Commencement of World War II. All services interrupted as ferry ships are dispersed onto war-time service. Post commandeered by Royal Naval personnel.
1945 -	May 8th -	V.E. DAY - Germans sign unconditional surrender.
	November 4th -	m.s. PRAGUE - arrives at Parkeston from war services.
	November 14th -	m.s. PRAGUE sails to Hook of Holland to re-commence post war service.
	December 12th -	m.s. PARKESTON first post war allied steamer to berth alongside Parkeston Quay.
1946 -	January 1st -	m.v. CITY OF MALINES sails to Antwerp.
	January 9th -	m.s. MECKLENBURG first post war Dutch vessel alongside Parkeston Quay.
	January 10th -	m.s. BATAVIA II - alongside Parkeston Quay.
	January 31st -	m.v. LYNN TRADER sails to Rotterdam.
	February 7th -	m.s. EMPIRE FABLE on Antwerp service.
	March 9th -	m.v. SHERINGHAM arrives at Parkeston Quay - demobilised.
	April 24th -	m.s. ORANGE NASSAU arrives at Parkeston Quay - ex Hook of Holland.
	May 26th -	m.s. KRONSPRINS FREDERIK arrives Parkeston Quay on her maiden voyage.
	August 16th -	m.v. ESSEX FERRY sails to commence post war train ferry sailing to Zeebrugge.
	August 27th -	m.v. DEWSBURY demobilised.
	September 20th -	m.v. FELIXSTOWE demobilised.
	November 25th -	m.s. NYENBURG sails to Flushing.

S.S. MECKLENBURG - post war - Note radar mast aft.

Troop ship S.S. EMPIRE PARKESTON

B.A.O.R.

(The following two articles are based on extracts from "The Harwich Standard", 1945)

Almost every day men of a dozen or more army units are to be seen strolling the streets of Harwich and Dovercourt. They are just a small part of the great Allied Army of Occupation of Europe; men of the B.A.O.R. who will never really lose their more popular title B.L.A. Day by day with amazing regularity ad efficiency the ships arrive and depart from Parkeston Quay bringing the men to England on eagerly anticipated leave and carrying them back away from parents and loved ones after a reunion that has seemed all too short.

The ordinary visitor to Parkeston Quay railway station can see much of the smooth efficiency which goes into the making of the vast organisation which ensures as near as possible trouble-free travel for these men of a great and victorious army, not forgetting their R.A.F. colleagues who travel to and fro with them.

In the early hours of the morning the ships arrive with their great human cargo. Landing formalities soon being over, special trains with N.A.A.F.I. buffet cars await and the men are whisked off untroubled by the problems of crowded trains and station queues to their destinations in all parts of the country.

Only a few hours later the special trains bringing the men back from leave start to arrive. There were four each day: two from London and two from the North. At the time each train is due a long line of lorries is ready waiting for the men. If the trains are late - as sometimes happens - the lorries wait. They are always there when the men arrive. The special train is signalled. Then men of the Military Police of Movement Control move into action. The R.T.O. Office stands by the deal with special problems. The trains run in, the men are conducted over the bridges - so that they shall not be delayed at the level crossing. Moving along the boundary of the station with their kit they bundle into the waiting lorries. The lorries carry the men to the Transit Camp - initially the Dovercourt Holiday Camp was used - and there the men are fed and rested and entertained, but mostly they find their way into the town. They are to be seen every day, men of almost every regiment and unit, displaying shoulder flashes that are frequently new, but often the well-known and familiar signs. They visit the shops, the cinemas, the pubs and the canteens. Then its back to the Transit Camp for a last meal and check-up. Finally they move into the lorries and back to Parkeston to board the ships for their crossing of the North Sea back to the continent which they stormed and won and which they now occupy as visitors and liberators.

That is the story of Harwich as a port of arrival and departure for the men of the B.A.O.R. - everyone still calls their train "the B.L.A." - and it is a traffic that is going on in many other ports, a traffic that is generally expected to continue at Harwich for many years to come.

It is a traffic which has led to the construction of the huge Army Transit Camp covering acres of land at Upper Dovercourt, which will eventually have complete accommodation for as many as 5,000 men, apart from the permanent staff.

TRANSIT CAMP

The fact that a million men have passed through Harwich going to and from their leave and that at the present rate another million will go through during the next twelve months is not only a matter of shipping; there is a shore establishment too, which plays an all important part in the programme, the 20 acre transit camp which the Army has built for itself at Dovercourt.

On a site where a year earlier green corn was billowing in the wind, today stands a great collection of buildings designed to house, feed and entertain anything up to 4,000 servicemen at a time.

Although local residents watched the growth of the camp with interest few have any idea of its size, its completeness or its efficiency. Most staggering of all perhaps are the amenities which it provides for the modern soldier.

The accommodation which the camp offers for the use of the men returning from leave and having to spend up to eleven or twelve hours in Harwich and Dovercourt pending the sailing of the leave ship, rivals that of any luxury holiday camp and competes with that of a first-rate hotel and restaurant.

Old time soldiers would shudder, the non-service person would be surprised and the serviceman would probably take for granted the magnificent lounges with attractive brick fire-places in modern style, furnished with massive leather settees and armchairs, the huge restaurant with its chromium and scarlet tables and chairs, the games rooms with their billiard tables, the dining halls and the washing accommodation. In fact everything is on a scale that requires a considerable adjustment of mind from the preconceived notion of an Army camp.

The work constructing the camp had been carried out under the direction of the Royal Engineers and considerable numbers of German prisoners of war have been engaged on the work, while civilian contractors have supplied materials and transport service.

As the camp neared completion the land that was a dreary stretch of mud a few months ago is being transformed. Trim green lawns, trees and shrubs are to be planted in front of the camp which will hide its harder lines and make it an attractive roadside picture at the entrance of the town.

There is a staff of about 300 engaged at the camp and a remarkable fact is that these men are drawn from 95 different Army units and are a constantly changing company as the various groups are released from service.

The transit camp was divided into two sections: that on the north side of the main Ramsey Road is devoted entirely to the accommodation of the permanent staff, while that on the opposite side of the road is for the B.A.O.R. leave personnel.

As a completely separate unit the staff section of the camp had its own store rooms and kitchen. The latter is beautifully clean with massive ranges and electric vegetable machines, designed to cope with the needs of 500 men and designed to ensure that officers and men get four good meals a day, breakfast, dinner, tea and supper. A typical breakfast menu offers porridge, cold ham and tea with the usual accessories; for dinner grilled liver and bacon, with vegetables, followed by mincemeat tart; for tea bully beef, bath buns; and then for supper whatever can be produced from the day's rations.

A particularly careful eye is kept on all food supplies to see that no waste occurs and a feature of every dining hall is a large sign - expertly painted by a sergeant of the staff - calling attention to the need for saving bread. These notices have made a tremendous difference to the waste of bread.

Special care is given to the education, welfare and recreation of the men attached to the camp staff. There are games rooms and comfortable messes, sports grounds and there is a fine handicraft room where the men can, in their off-duty hours, follow any natural bent in practical work. Many well-finished articles in wood and in the new glass-like material perspex are made.

There is a well equipped educational office and every member of the staff has to do six hours study each week. A wide range of subjects are covered and this aspect of Army life is considered particularly important for men on the point of being released, equipping them for a return to civilian life and employment. In addition to the more academic subjects there is a wide range of practical studies such as woodwork, household repairs, light metal work and boot repairing. For their vocation training men are encouraged to obtain practical experience with local firms of builders and plumbers and the commanding officer welcomes offers from employers who provide facilities for the men. In addition instructors who are prepared to devote some spare time to instructing the men in these subjects are also utilised. Quite a number of the men qualify for the Army's Formation College at Luton where they are trained to instruct fellow soldiers whilst in the Army and also on leaving the Forces. In addition a re-settlement officer from the Ministry of Labour and National Service visits the camp each week to give personal attention to the men's individual problems as they approach their release.

Also important from an educational point of view is the fine selection of reference books that was available in the library, which also provided fiction reading varying from the heaviest to the light. Each day one of the camp's officers led a discussion group on a topical subject at which the men are encouraged to express their views.

About one and a half acres of land are being devoted to growing vegetables to meet the camp's requirements as far as possible, while all round the building which comprises the camp, flower beds and lawns are laid out. A mass of tubular steel work which has formed invasion defence is being used to rail off the paths and when painted white will provide a very trim and neat finish to the appearance of the camp. Tennis courts are also laid out.

On the staff side of the camp is the Casualty Reception Station. The name covers what is in effect a miniture hospital, beautifully fitted and equipped, although all serious and surgical cases are sent to the military hospital at Colchester. In this reception station men of the camp staff and men who are taken ill while travelling to and from leave are cared for. The hospital has its own kitchen where the meals for the patients are prepared and any special diets can be provided.

The section of the camp devoted to the men of the B.A.O.R. is on the same grand scale, with everything multiplied to cope with the increased numbers. As the men arrive back from leave by the special trains they are conveyed from Parkeston station to the camp by Army lorries and on arrival their baggage is stacked. They receive all necessary instructions. The canteens and restaurants are open to them and their meals are served. There is every possible entertainment, including a cinema. All the men have to do for themselves is to fill in the few hours until they are taken off by lorry once again to the leave ships. As the day goes and further special trains arrive the camp gradually fills up, but in spite of the big numbers to be dealt with, the whole camp is cleared by lorries in one and a half hours once the leave personnel start "en-bussing" for the quay.

Should a hold-up of any kind occur there are beds available for all leave personnel and they can be fed and looked after until the ships are ready to leave. Men who have travelled all night from distant parts have a bed available as soon as they reach the camp and can "turn-in" for the afternoon if they wish.

The lounges and game rooms provided for the leave personnel have literally, to be seen to be believed. Imagine a huge hotel lounge with armchairs and settees in gay red leather, a brick fireplace, a bar in the corner, gaily covered floors, pictures on the walls and curtains at the windows, books to read, radio and small tables and chairs scattered about. That is something of the picture.

The restaurant, with seating for 750 men, is a picture of modernity. Scarlet and chromium chairs and tables stretch in a line that seems never to end. Serving hatches in light oak colour run down one side of the room. This is all a N.A.A.F.I. service, but very far removed from the old idea of a service canteen. The restaurant has the latest form of air-conditioned heating and the kitchens have steam cooking apparatus.

The camp has its own complete Post Office operated by regular Post Office staff and scattered about the camp are numerous telephone boxes; not the gaunt red affairs of the street, but quiet efficient affairs tucked away into corners in hotel style.

Every taste is catered for and the Army's beer was available in the "Tavern" a lofty room with simulated oak beams to give an atmosphere of the "pub".

No charge is made to the men for any of the facilities which the camp provided. A huge baggage room will store all the men's equipment while they are in the camp.

For officers staying in the camp there are separate cubicles. Otherwise the facilities and food for both officers and "other ranks" are almost identical and the camp provides an insight into the really democratic Army which Britain has developed during the past few years.

About 30 German prisoners-of-war were on the staff of the camp and act as gardeners and kitchen orderlies and are generally regarded as good workers. One prisoner with an artistic bent is busily engaged on decorating all the general rooms of the camp, painting delightful pictures direct on the cream distempered walls. The boiler house which provides the camp with hot water and heating is manned by 25 ex-naval stokers.

In the store rooms and kitchens everything is scrupolously clean. Spraying of D.D.T. has put an end to the fly menace.

The camp is a wonderful achievement and looking back over a visit the visitor must come to the conclusion that the British Army has travelled a very long way from the so-called "good old days". The camp is an example of the care which is taken for the bodily and mental welfare of the soldier of today, caring for him while he is in the Army and preparing him for his return to the "rigours of civilian life". So far as the leave personnel are concerned it rounds off all the hard corners and makes as pleasant as it can be the duty which required a man to leave his home and dear ones and travel at regular intervals to distant lands to live among his ex-enemies.

S.S. SHERINGHAM
Built 1926, she served pre-war as a cargo ship. During the 1939-45 war she served under the Ministry of War Transport, after which she resumed her career from Harwich. She was sold to Belgium shipbreakers on 21st December, 1958.

Loading cattle for export onto the S.S. SHERINGHAM
Last export of livestock at Parkeston Quay - 1951.

S.S. PRAGUE - as an Army Ambulance ship during World War II

T.S.S. PRAGUE
Sister ship to the "AMSTERDAM" (II) and "VIENNA" (II) with whom she served on the pre 1939-45 war Harwich-Hook service. After a distinguished war career for the American Forces, she reverted to her peace time role re-opening the Hook service in 1945. Whilst undergoing reconditioning at Clydebank in 1947, she was damaged by fire and finally broken up at Barrow.

1947 - January 17th - m.s. ZWERVER sails to Flushing.
       January 18th - m.s. MARCEL
       May 12th - s.s. ARNHEM arrives at Parkeston Quay.
       May 28th - s.s. ARNHEM sails on maiden voyage to Hook of Holland.
       September 3rd - m.s. SUFFOLK FERRY joins Zeebrugge Train Ferry service.
1948 - January 1st - LNER nationalised. Running of Parkeston Quay assumed by British Transport Authority.
1949 - June 14th - m.s. KRONPRISESSE INGRID - arrives at Parkeston Quay on maiden voyage.
1950 - February 1st - m.v. DEWSBURY left Parkeston on her last voyage to Antwerp.
       February 1st - m.v. ACCRINGTON left Parkeston on her last voyage to Antwerp.
       May 29th - m.s. AMSTERDAM arrives at Parkeston to enter Harwich-Holland service.
1953 - January 31st - Period of floods over district.
       February 2nd - All services suspended.
       April 19th - DFDS vessel - KRONSPRINS FREDERIK - fire.
       May 6th - m.v. DUKE OF YORK collides with m.v. HAITI VICTORY.
                       m.v. NORMANIA borrowed from Southern Region to bridge the gap.

S.S. VIENNA
on her maiden voyage

Burnt out wreck of

M.S. KRONSPRINS FREDERIK

S.S. ACCRINGTON
One of a family of five sister ships built for the old Great Central Railway. Was transferred to the Harwich-Antwerp service in 1946 as a cargo/passenger ship until 1950, thereafter as a cargo ship until scrapped in 1951.

S.S. DEWSBURY
Along with the "ACCRINGTON" was transferred to Harwich in 1946 to supplement war losses. She served on the Antwerp route, until sold to Dutch breakers in February, 1959.

T.S.S. AMSTERDAM (III)
Built by John Brown & Co., Glasgow, with her sister ship "ARNHEM". She carried first and second class passengers, with sleeping accommodation for 557 passengers. Came into the Harwich-Hook service 13th June, 1950.

T.S.S. ARNHEM

First vessel of the Harwich fleet ordered by the British Transport Commission. Came into service as a first class ship, May 1947. Was converted in 1954, and with increased accommodation carried 584 first and second class passengers. She was the first Harwich vessel fitted for oil burning.

Came into the Harwich (Parkeston Quay) Hook of Holland route in May 1947 for first class passengers.

Such is the close spirit of Anglo-Dutch relationship that the S.S. ARNHEM, named after a famous and heroic district of Holland was launched by the wife of H.E. the Nederlands Ambassador in London on 8th November, 1948.

After 21 years service, the ship was scrapped in August 1968.

T.S.S. DUKE OF YORK

Was commissioned by the London Midland Region in 1935, it being the second vessel of this name with the Company. Served during the 1939-45 war as H.M.S. WELLINGTON.

On January 1st, 1949 was transferred to join the "ARNHEM" on the Harwich-Hook service. She was extensively altered in 1950 by having a large number of additional berths fitted and converted to oil burning. After her collision with the American ship "HAITI VICTORY" in May 1953, she was taken to Jarrow on Tyne; was given a new bow and lengthened by about seven feet. She rejoined the Harwich fleet early 1954 to be used mainly as a relief ship. She was sold to Greek owners in August 1963, being re-registered as "YORK OF MONROVIA", and later named "FANTASIA".

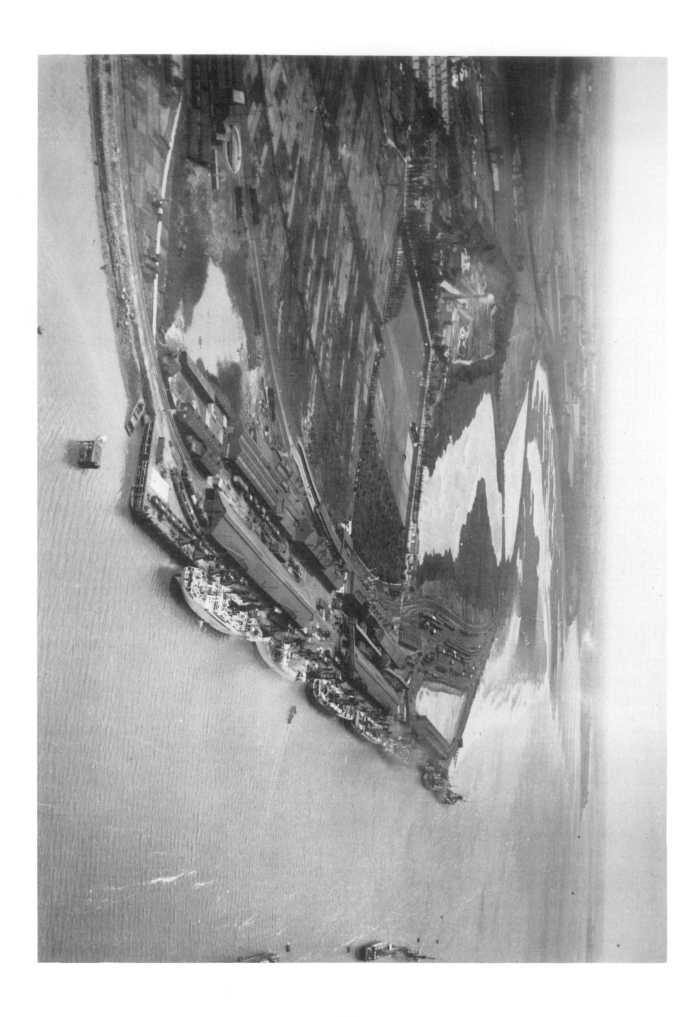

Shots of the damaged "DUKE OF YORK"

M.V. COLCHESTER (II)
Came into service 2nd February 1959. Sister ship to the "ISLE OF ELY" - both built for the Harwich-Rotterdam/Harwich-Antwerp cargo service to replace the steamers "ACCRINGTON" and "DEWSBURY". Designed to carry general cargo, they were altered in 1968 to take standard high capacity containers in cellular holds. She was the first vessel to appear in the new British Rail colours.

M.V. ISLE OF ELY
Although a "twin" in all respects to that of her sister the "COLCHESTER", she came into service on 27th October, 1958; and like that of her sister ship was altered in 1968 to take standard high capacity containers.

1954 -   ARNHEM and AMSTERDAM (III) on Hook route with DUKE OF YORK, returned from repair yards.

1956 -   Services to Antwerp suspended.

1958 -   March 22nd -   Royal Yacht BRITTANIA arrives with HRH THE QUEEN before departing for trip to Holland.

        October 27th -   "ISLE OF ELY" - first trip to Rotterdam.

1959 -   January 24th -   COLCHESTER commences service to Antwerp.

1960 -   Koningin Wilhelmina on maiden voyage run from the Hook.

1961 -   BAOR ships finish service.

1963 -   s.s. AVALON arrives at Parkeston Quay.

1964 -   January 1st -   NAVYARD opened for service.

        January 2nd -   VIKING III arrives at the Navyard.

        January 3rd -   m.v. TRAVIALTA unloads first cargo of trade cars.

        April 24th -   AVALON goes on her first cruise.

        June 11th -   m.s. ENGLAND arrives at Parkeston Quay on maiden voyage.

1966 -   May 24th -   New service to Bremerhaven commenced today. m.s. SOMERSET first DFDS RO/RO cargo vessel.

1967 -   May 18th -   BLACK PRINCE commenced service to Kristiansands.

        June 8th -   Refrigerated bacon trailer service commenced by m.s. STAFFORD.

        June 9th -   m.s. STAFFORD. RO/RO bacon trailer ship arrives from Esbjerg.

1968 -   March 17th -   SEA FREIGHTLINER I - arrives alongside Container Terminal.

        May 1st -   Passenger and RO/RO services ran by Belgium Rail/Sea System to Ostend. Service only ran to 1972.

        June 3rd -   SEA FREIGHTLINER II - arrives alongside Container terminal.

        July 17th -   m.v. ST. GEORGE - maiden voyage to Hook.

        August 13th -   ARNHEM left to breakers yard.

        October 17th -   KONINGIN JULIANA arrives at Parkeston Quay on maiden voyage.

        December 31st - BREMERHAVEN service transferred to Navyard.

M.S. KONINGIN WILHELMINA

M.S. SUFFOLK - Actually berthed on the West Portal

NAVYARD WHARF - pre 1964

NAVYARD WHARF - 1970

NAVYARD WHARF - 1964

NAVYARD WHARF - 1970

1969 -	January 1st -	Formation of SEALINK
1971 -	May 29th -	m.v. BLENHEIM on Kristiansand service.
1972 -	March 28th -	WINSTON CHURCHILL alongside in new DFDS livery.
	May 16th -	New passenger terminal building at car park officially opened.
1974 -	July 9th -	m.s. DANA REGINA arrives at Parkeston Quay on her maiden voyage.
	December 24th -	m.v. ST. EDMUND arrives at Parkeston Quay for her maiden voyage.
	December 29th -	AVALON leaves Parkeston Quay for convertion to RO/RO service.
1975 -	January 19th -	m.v. ST. EDMUND maiden voyage to Hook of Holland.
1975 -	Centenary of the S.M.Z.	
1978 -	May 6th -	m.s. DANA ANGLIA arrives alongside the Quay.
	June 29th -	m.s. PRINCESS BEATRIX arrives alongside the Quay on her maiden voyage.
1979 -	January 1st -	PRINS LINES Ferries return to operating German service from Parkeston Quay.

1980 -	June 4th -	DFDS celebrate century of service of the Harwich-Esbjerg service.
1981 -	September 1st -	DFDS take control of Prins Lines Ferries.
	September 2nd -	PRINZ OBERON appears in new DFDS/PRINS LINES colours.
1982 -	June 12th -	m.v. ST. EDMUND sails to join Falklands Task Force.
1983 -	March 15th -	Sealink commemorate the centenary of the opening of Parkeston Quay.
	April 1st -	m.v. TOR SCANDINAVIA arrives from Gothenburg - return of Gothenburg/Harwich service by TOR-LINES.
	June 10th -	m.v. ST. NICHOLAS joins the SEALINK fleet.
1984 -	July 30th -	SEALINK PRIVATISED.
1985 -	June 10th -	Service to Oslo by the Fred Olsen line.
1986 -	April 22nd -	KONINGIN BEATRIX arrives on maiden voyage.

Loading export trade cars. M.V. TRAVIALTO at the Navyard Wharf

M.S. WINSTON CHURCHILL in the Company's new livery

M.S. SUFFOLK - Before being lengthened

M.S. SUSSEX - Before being lengthened

1971 - AUGUST 5th

The biggest Roll-on/Roll-off Cargo ship to berth at Harwich arrived at Parkeston Quay on her maiden voyage.

She is the "CARIBBEAN ENDEAVOUR"; 5,300 tons dead weight and is on a charter to the Danish Shipping Line DFDS.

She had been chartered for four months as a stand-in while other DFDS ships such as the "SOMERSET" and the "SUFFOLK" go into dock.

Normally these smaller vessels operate from Newcastle and Grimsby but the "CARIBBEAN ENDEAVOUR" is too big for these ports. Therefore DFDS decided to put her into Harwich, transferring the smaller "SUFFOLK" which normally operates the Harwich/Esbjerg run to Newcastle and into Grimsby for the four months of the dry-docking period.

The m.v. "CARIBBEAN ENDEAVOUR" is a German ship capable of carrying 93 forty foot trailers on three decks. She has bow thrust and variable pitch propellers controlled from the bridge. The Bridge is so far from the engine room that 123 steps has to be climbed from one point to the other.

M.S. STAFFORD - After being lenghtened

S.S. AVALON (III)
When this vessel came into the Harwich-Hook service, she was the largest owned by the British Railways and was the first British cross-channel ship to be fitted throughout with a full air-conditioning system. Commissioned in 1963, apart from the regular service, she had been used as a cruise ship. She now serves Sealink on another route. The name Avalon is derived from the island to which the mythical King Arthur was conveyed for the healing of his wounds after his final battle and from which he never returned.

The identification of Avalon with Glastonbury (Somerset) may have been based on Celtic stories about a 'summer land' inhabited by deceased heroes.

M.S. SURREY

PARKESTON QUAY CONTAINER TERMINAL

The use of containers is as old as the wooden box, which has been developed throughout the years in various shapes and forms. Its recent development is due to the shipping lines of the world adopting universal standard units, termed ISO Containers.

Great Britain was one of the first countries to adopt this concept, and British Rail created the 'Freightliner' system of Container Trains, giving direct access between industrial centres in the United Kingdom and certain container ports. Every week-day direct container trains arrive at Parkeston.

It was in 1965 that British Rail decided to start a container service between Harwich and continental ports, with special ships of cellular structure to enable the transport of containers in units of 20, 30 and 40ft lengths.

The service from Harwich started in early 1968 with routes to Rotterdam and Zeebrugge. To serve the Rotterdam route, two Dutch ships were utilised (the m.v. "DOMBURGH" and m.v. "NASSUA") whilst the Zeebrugge service utilised two British Rail vessels (the m.v. "COLCHESTER" and m.v. "ISLE OF ELY") which had been specially converted, from carrying general cargoes, to the conveyance of ISO containers.

17th March, 1968, saw the arrival of the first of two new container ships, the m.v. "SEAFREIGHTLINER I". Its arrival greatly intensified the service between Harwich and Zeebrugge. When her sister ship, m.v. "SEAFREIGHTLINER II", arrived on the service, the "COLCHESTER" and "ISLE OF ELY" were withdrawn. The m.v. "COLCHESTER", can now be seen on the Liverpool-Spain/Portugal route of Messrs. MacAndrews.

Such was the success of this service, that in its first year of operation 21,000 containers were shipped to Zeebrugge, a figure which jumped to 65,000 in 1969, with both the Seafreightliner ships each doing a daily Harwich/Zeebrugge return trip.

This service ceased to operate; December 1985.

M.V. SEAFREIGHTLINER I

M.V. SEAFREIGHTLINER II

These two container ships operate the service between Harwich and Zeebrugge and were the first of their type to be built in Britain. The containers slot into cell spaces in sectionised holds, occupying the whole of the cargo space. Each ship can make one round trip per day. Built in South Shields, they entered the service in 1968.

M.V. GEORGE

Prior to the arrival of the "ST. EDMUND", this vessel was the largest ship in the Sealink fleet a clear indication of the importance attached by the railways to the maintainence of the Harwich-Hook service. Her service is still utilised at Parkeston to ensure the service is fully operated throughout the year.

St. George, Patron Saint of England, was a Roman Centurion, who, upon becoming a Christian, took up his sword in defence of his faith and with other Christians battled against Roman troops of the Legion who bore a dragon as their emblem. Hence the reason St. George is always depicted fighting a dragon.

M.S. BLACK WATCH

T.S.M.V. PRINSES JOSEPHINE CHARLOTTE

T.S.M.V. ARTEVELDE

T.S.M.V. KONINGIN FABIOLA

T.S.M.V. ROI BAUDOUIN

T.S.M.V. PRINCESSE ASTRID

1984 - APRIL 24th

Today sees the Harwich/Zeebrugge train ferry service and Anglo-Belgian partnership celebrate its Diamond anniversary. This Anglo-Belgian partnership has been running the Train Ferry service from a special terminal in Harwich to Zeebrugge now for sixty years. Train Ferries 1, 2 and 3 operated the route until the outbreak of hostilities in the second World War when they were requisitioned and used to transport raw materials between Harwich and Calais. Train Ferry Number 2 was sunk at St. Valery in 1940 and Number 3 struck a mine and sunk in March 1945. Train Ferry 1, commissioned as H.M.S. "PRINCESS IRIS" was reconstructed as a Train Ferry in 1946 renamed the "ESSEX FERRY" and re-opened the Zeebrugge service the same year. She was joined by the "Suffolk Ferry" in 1947 and the "Norfolk Ferry" in 1951. The "Essex Ferry" was herself replaced by a new ship bearing the same name in 1957. The fourth ferry "CAMBRIDGE" entered the Service in 1964. The "Suffolk Ferry" was replaced in September 1980, by the Swedish Ro-Ro vessel "Stenna Shipper", later renamed the "Speedlink Vanguard". Since 1985 the "Speedlink Vanguard" is the mainstay of the route with only the "Cambridge Ferry" still remaining. In 1982 the "Essex" and "Norfolk" were both laid up. The "Norfolk" finally went to Holland as scrap and the "Essex" was sold to a Norwegian Company who used her as a Pontoon to assist in the raising of a capsized oil platform.

With the transfer of the "CAMBRIDGE FERRY", during December 1986 - this service is due to be moved to Dover by the end of Janaury 1987.

We discovered references to the Victorian crane which was built for the Great Eastern Railway Company whilst researching our Harwich: A Nautical History Book. We discovered that the crane with a hoist load of about thirty-three hundred weight was being used at the Harwich Train Ferry Terminal - although for a purpose other than it was originally intended.

The crane is the last surviving example of its kind still in railway service in the country and that it had originally stood in the Harwich Goods Depot.

It was used there to assist men moving heavy loads from rail wagons for more than a century until 1968. It was then left for two years before being dismantled, taken to the B.R. workshops at Parkeston Quay and renovated. Two years ago it was re-erected at the waters edge at the Train Ferry Terminal. Its main function nowadays is to raise and lower machinery and timbers onto a raft, which is then towed into position around the terminal structure while repairs are carried out.

T.S.M.V. KONINGIN ELIZABETH

Train Ferry No. 1 shown after post-war reconstruction and renamed ESSEX FERRY (I)

ESSEX FERRY (II)

SUFFOLK FERRY

NORFOLK FERRY

CAMBRIDGE FERRY

1980 - SEPTEMBER

The "Stenna Shipper" has been chartered for service on the Harwich-Zeebrugge train ferry route. Renamed "Speed Vanguard" she will provide additional capacity for railborne freight from September 1980 and the entry into later service of two newly built, large train ferries for which it is hoped approval will be given during the next few months.

Last year the Train Ferry Services from Harwich to Zeebrugge and Dunkirk carried almost 500,000 tons of railborne freight, an increase of 80,000 tons on 1978 figures.

M.V. SPEEDLINK VANGUARD
At present operating, with the Cambridge ferry acting as reserve, on the Harwich-Zeebrugge Train Ferry route

M.S. KONINGIN JULIANA

1968 - JULY 17th

With the arrival of the "Koningin Juliana' which was similar in design to the 'St. George' the British ship has left Parkeston at noon and returned from the Hook at 23.15 hrs., while the Dutch ship has left Holland at 11.30 hrs., to return from Parkeston at 22.00 hrs.

1971 - JUNE 4th

The "BLENHEIM" arrived at Parkeston Quay last Saturday. The 13,000 ton ship sailed later in the afternoon on her twenty-two hour voyage to Kristiansand with 600 passengers.

1972 - FEBRUARY 25th

A Goliath Crane was floated across the Baltic and the North Sea to land at Harwich from Finland today. It had been ordered from the Finnish crane manufacturers KONE by the British Railways Board for service at Parkeston Quay.

The crane was completed at Kone's HANKO works on the southern most tip of Finland. From Hanko it was fully transported and ready for operation on a pontoon. It reached Harwich about February and a few days later it was winched from the pontoon to Parkeston Quay, using provisional rails. The exact day depended upon the weather conditions.

Computers had calculated how much a crane can toss about at sea without danger. An alarm light showed on this towing tug if there was excessible tossing, and the tug would head for shelter or alter course to reduce the motion. The Finnish manufacturers have delivered several other cranes by this method.

The crane has a total weight of 270 tons and a span of 75 feet. The hoisting capacity under the spreader is 30 tons.

1974 - JULY 9th
M.S. DANA REGINA - Alongside Parkeston Quay on her maiden voyage.
DFDS Building in fore-ground also houses the office of the Danish Vice-Consul

1974 - JUNE

The quarter of a million pound scheme to give better facilities for motorists at Harwich (Parkeston Quay) has been officially opened. Improvements include an additional hard standing assembling area for out-going cars and an over-bridge between the assembling area and loading ramp. Cars formerly used a nearby level-crossing to reach the ships but British Rail's continued increase in passenger traffic has meant delays were fairly obvious. The new overhead complex will help eliminate this and give motorists a fair deal.

1975 - JANUARY 19th
M.V. ST. EDMUND leaving on maiden voyage to the Hook of Holland

M.V. ST. EDMUND
Was launched at Cammell Laird's shipyard, Birkenhead in November 1973. Named after a ninth century King of East Anglia, the 9,000 ton vessel cost about £7.5 million. She entered the Harwich-Hook service on January 21st 1975. Was chartered May 11th 1982 by H.M. Government for service with the Falkland Islands Task Force.

1978 - MAY 6th
M.S. DANA ANGLIA - arrives alongside Parkeston Quay

1976 - JANUARY 16th

The latest addition to the DFDS fleet the "Dana Futura" has arrived at Parkeston Quay. The new Ro/Ro ferry is the first of two ships on order for DFDS from the Elsingborge Shipbuilding and Engineering Company Limited. The "Dana Futura" and her sister ship which has still to be launched - the "Dana Gloria" - are the largest Ro/Ro Cargo Ferries to be built in Denmark. They should be seen regularly on the Esbjerg - Harwich (Parkeston Quay) Ferry service in the future.

1976

In the Freight world the company's (DFDS) increase in capacity is shown by the fact that in the "Dana Gloria" five round trips this year she carried as much as cargo as the whole of the DFDS fleet in 1900.

1977 - MAY

Confident comments were expressed that the trade car traffic through the Hook of Holland - Harwich (Parkeston Quay) will continue to grow during this year. Last year, traffic was so prominent that most normal car ferry services carried some trade cars. Train Ferry "Essex Ferry" made a number of special sailings between the Hook and Harwich to clear backlogs and Zeeland Steamship Company chartered at least on two occasions, private vessels in order to keep the flow moving. At one stage the Hook of Holland Port Complex became saturated with trade cars.

1977 - SEPTEMBER

This past season has seen a growth of traffic by the Sealink services of caravans. These are received from 5 manufacturers in the Hull area exporting this form of traffic to the Continent by the Harwich train ferry service. Two years ago the majority of their traffic was shipped by the Humber Ports, but then Sealink Salesmen became armed with more attractive rates and traffic was run by the Harwich Ferry Services. This service now sees around thirty-five or so caravans shipped every week. A proportion of this traffic is likewise shipped through Parkeston Quay on the Hook of Holland Route.

1980 - JANUARY

Ford Motor Company has increased its flow of imported trade cars through Parkeston Quay from 400 to 600 cars per day. The cars arrive at the Quay from France, Belgium and Germany.

1980 - JUNE 4th

Today saw the centenary of the Danish connection between Esbjerg and Harwich. But it was in 1849 that a boat belonging to a company which was eventually to form part of DFDS made a one off trip into Harwich Harbour. She was the "CITY OF NORWICH" and ths firm was the Continental Cattle Conveyancing Co.

Det Forende Dampskips Selskab began services between the Danish port of Esbjerg and Harwich and Newcastle with live cattle for trade. At the time passengers took second place. One could make a crossing for as little as 20p - the same price as a pig. But it would take and extra £1.50 for you to buy covered accommodation. And even then one had to provide ones own cutlery and plates for the food which was charged for as an extra. One thing would no doubt be popular nowadays - the Company gave free beer.

1982 - NOVEMBER

The new Tor Line and Freight Services, currently operating out of Felixstowe, will need a deepening of the existing link-span berth at Parkeston Quay enabling it to accommodate traffic of ships up to 7.5 metres draught. The work that Parkeston will need, will cost five million pounds.

This also includes the provision of additional storage facilities. DFDS, who now own Tor Lines, as well as Prins Ferries, has a near monopoly of UK/Scandinavian passenger services as well as a major share of the freight business. The transfer to Parkeston Quay will provide Tor Line passengers with direct access to our services to London with an eighty-three minutes journey time.

Limited works will be carried out at the East Portal Berth at Parkeston Quay to accommodate the Tor Line multi-purpose service from the 1st April on a temporary basis until completion of the new berth due May 1984.

1983 - APRIL 1st

The ''Tor Britannia'', berthed at Parkeston Quay, for the first time helped the port to break all previous passenger records. More than 13,000 passengers travelled through Parkeston Quay on March 31st - a record for any day in the Port.

The 15,673 ton ''Tor Britannia'' arrived from Gothenburg with 1,330 passengers. DFDS Tor Lines passengers terminal - Felixstowe, has now closed and all passengers will now use Parkeston Quay.

1983 - FEBRUARY

Confirmation that DFDS are to switch their TOR Line services to Gothenburg from Felixstowe to Parkeston Quay was reported today. The service which begins on April 1st will also mean job security at the Quay, although it is not yet known whether more jobs will be created locally. Better passenger and freight facilities make the Quay more attractive. At Parkeston, passengers will have direct access to London Rail services although, with local sightseeing. Two ferries, the "TOR BRITANNIA" and "TOR SCANDINAVIA" will be used on the run during the peak summer period.

DFDS took over the flagging Tor Line in 1981.

1984 - JULY 30th

Sea Containers Limited today completed its acquisition of Sealink UK Limited. The Premier British Ferry Company operating a Fleet of 37 ships over 24 routes and owning ten Harbours. The Sealink U.K. shares will be held by British Ferries Limited a U.K. wholly owned subsidiary of Sea Containers Limited. The purchase price was sixty-six million pounds. In 1983 Sealink U.K. had net income of 6.4 million on Revenue of 265 million pounds.

1985 - JUNE 1st

Overleaf is shown a photograph of the m.s. "BRAEMAR", Fred Olsen's new Luxury ship introduced onto the Harwich/Norwegian route. At 14,300 tons, she has a capacity for 2,000 passengers and 486 cars. For the past few years Fred Olsin has been running a service from Harwich to Kristiansands. Now Norway is back on the map on all year basis following the news that the Harwich (Parkeston Quay) to Kristiansands route has been a great success. The weekly run to Hirtshals in North Jutland continues onto Oslo and operates all year round.

m.s. "BRAEMAR" is one of the huge new super ferries the North Sea has been getting over the past few years and each carrying about 2,000 passengers plus nearly 500 cars, with a registered tonnage of plus 14,000.

The "BRAEMAR" is typically Scandinavian. It has an amazing tropic garden lounge, a sauna bath, a swimming pool and to quote the modern idiom even possesses its own jogging track. What would pass off as a Duty Free shop on most ships is called on the "BRAEMAR" supermarket, it sells spirits at slightly higher prices than in British High Street shops, which for Norwegians must sound very reasonable.

It is intersting to note that Kristiansands even at the higher altitude to the extreme North of Scotland, reliably has the Gulf Stream to keep the region much warmer than elsewhere in the North. The water amid the scurries on the approaches to Kristiansands is warmer in July than any resort in normal temperatures. It is also a fact that the sea water of Oslo Fjords is the warmest from early July to mid August of any sea waters in Europe outside the Mediterranean. But, be warned, by the end of August the short, hot summer has given away to an Autumn which soon deepens to an eight months winter. However so popular is Norway, that the Olsen line are again running m.v. "BOULERS" on the Summer 1986 season.

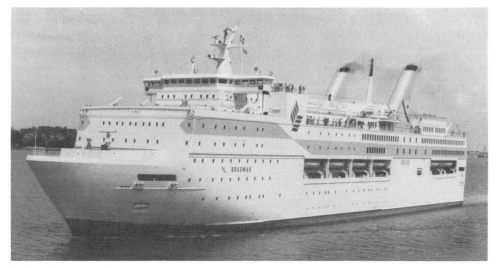

M.V. BRAEMAR

The new link-span in operation

A SAINT ARRIVES

HUGE CROWDS LINED HARWICH QUAY to welcome the new addition to the Sealink fleet. The m.v. "St. Nicholas" with Capt. Fred Wilkins on the bridge, steered into harbour ablaze with lights. This massive vessel steamed up river to dock by Parkeston Quay just after 10 pm.

Formerly name the "Prinsessan Birgitta", this Swedish built ferry, completed last year by Gotaverken, Gothenburg, was originally laid down for Stera Line, but later chartered by Sealink for a five year period; Sealink renamed the ferry the "St. Nicholas" and as such she takes over from their other two ferries - the "St. George" (who is awaiting a buyer) and the "St. Edmund" (sold to the Defence Ministry) - the Harwich-Hook route.

Some of the technical details of this vessel are as follows:-

G.R. Tonnage	14,368 tons
Overall length	489 feet
Passengers	500 1st class
	1,600 2nd class
No of Car spaces	480
Space for lorries	52 x 15 mtrs.
Service Speed	20 knots
Total, engine	21,000 (h.p.)

Realising that boredom is the main factor of the 6 hour day-time crossing, Sealink have had installed a cinema, showing the latest films, with a programme change of 3 showings on the day crossing and 2 showings on the night crossing. It is stated that there is also a roulette and blackjack table in the Terrace Bar. As well as the usual Duty Free shopping facilities, the ship also has 3 conference areas.

Although flying the Swedish flag when entering the Port - she now flies the Red Ensign with British Officer and crew - and is re-registered in London.

The m.v. "St. Nicholas" made her maiden voyage - Parkeston Quay to the Hook of Holland on Friday June 10th and a ceremony was held on Wednesday 15th June, when Mrs. B. Henderson, wife of Sealink U.K.'s deputy Managing Director, and a former Shipping Manager at Parkeston Quay - named this ship.

M.V. ST. NICHOLAS

M.V. PRINSES BEATRIX

FROM A PRINCESS TO A QUEEN

1986 - APRIL 22nd

The ''Koningin Beatrix'', the new Flag Ship of the Stoomvaart Maatschappij Zeeland, was built by the Van de Giessen de Noord shipyard, thus proving that it is not for nothing that the Dutch shipping industry ranks among the very best in the world.

A tremendous display of craftmanship resulting in the most modern vessel ever to sail between Holland and Harwich - Parkeston Quay.

All the former pleasures characteristic of sea travel have come back with this new ship which was transformed the ''Beatrix'' from a Princess into a Queen. The ship that provides incontrovertible proof that sailing is the most stylish method of travel. This vessel replaces the Princess Beatrix which will disappear from her familiar role between Harwich and the Hook of Holland, the Koningin Beatrix takes place, for this is the largest and finest passenger and car ferry vessel ever to maintain a daily service over this route. All the knowledge and all the expertise of more than a hundred years have been incorporated into this rather imposing looking ship.

M.V. KONINGIN BEATRIX

We close as we opened this book - LONGSHIPS - in and out of the River Stour and onto the North Sea.

Above is the m.s. "TOR BRITANNIA" - seen in the company's latest colour ... from overleaf are photographs (courtesy of the World Ship Society) of a few of the many motorised "Longships" that have traversed the by now familiar ESBJERG/HARWICH ferry route. The figure in brackets after the ships name is the year in which the vessel operated on the service.

S.S. J.C. JACOBSEN (1890)

S.S. DAGMAR (1920)

S.S. CHRISTIAN (1875)

S.S. N.J. FJORD (1896)

S.S. TYR (1900)

S.S. DRONING MAULD (1906)

S.S. KONG HAAKON (1906)

S.S. FLORA (1909)

S.S. VIDAR (1915)

S.S. THYRA (1923)

S.S. ROTA (1923)

S.S. ALEXANDRA (1931)

S.S. TRONDHJEM (1923)

M.S. TUNIS (1936)

M.S. ESBJERG (1929)

M.S. MAROCCO (1936)

S.S. BERGENHUS (1922)

M.S. FICARIA (1951)

M.S. PRIMULA (1952)

M.S. ENGLAND (1964)

M.S. KRONPRINSESSE INGRID (1949)

Above, berthed at Esbjerg

Below, berthed at Parkeston Quay

M.S. SUFFOLK (1966)

M.S. SUSSEX (1966)

M.S. DANA GERMANIA (1985)

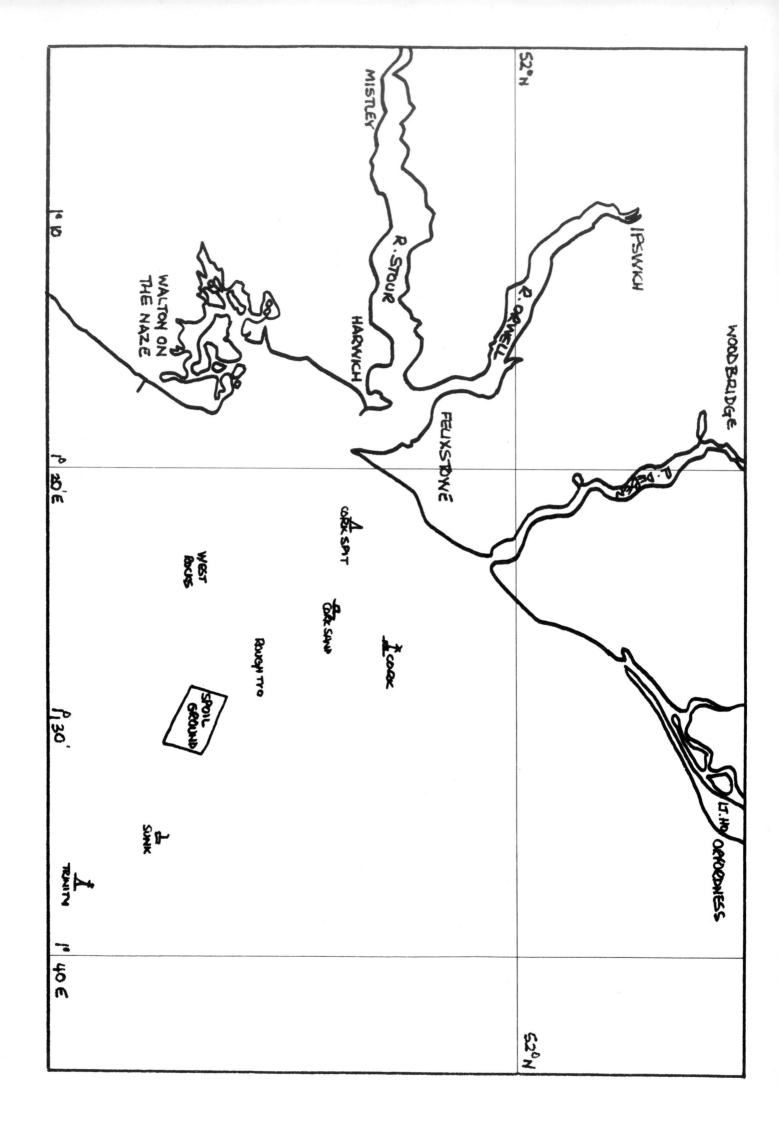

A Body
in the
Bookshop

Helen Cox is a Yorkshire-born novelist and poet. After completing her MA in creative writing at the University of York St John, Helen wrote for a range of magazines and websites as well as for TV and radio news. Helen has edited her own independent film magazine and penned three non-fiction books, and her first two novels were published by HarperCollins in 2016. She currently hosts The Poetry-gram podcast and works for City Lit, London. Helen's new series of cozy mysteries stars librarian-turned-sleuth Kitt Hartley, and is set in York.

Helen's Mastermind specialism would be *Grease 2* and to this day she adheres to the Pink Lady pledge. More information about Helen can be found on her website: helencoxbooks.com, or on Twitter: @Helenography.

THE KITT HARTLEY YORKSHIRE MYSTERIES

Murder by the Minster
A Body in the Bookshop